HOLY VOID

Zero-Thought-Consciousness

YAREK ALFER

Edited by Catherine Bogart

Published by GFB™, Seattle
www.girlfridayproductions.com

Produced by Girl Friday Productions

Design: Paul Barrett
Production editorial: Alyssa Brillinger
Project management: Kristin Duran

ISBN (paperback): 978-1-964721-50-7
ISBN (ebook): 978-1-964721-49-1

Library of Congress Control Number: 2025902146

First edition

CONTENTS

PREFACE

My Lifelong Study of Advaita

I think that for some readers it may be of interest to know a few pertinent details about my lifelong study of Advaita. I will start with relevant events in my childhood.

At age four I received my first "religious" instructions in a Soviet Siberian Gulag. The kindergarten teacher routinely made us stand at attention in front of Stalin's portrait while she recited praises to the almighty *batushka* (dear holy father) Stalin who is in Moscow, giving us our daily bread (I am paraphrasing).

The Second World War and the deportation with my parents to the Siberian Gulag disrupted my bucolic childhood. The resulting confusion was felt during my early schooling and university studies for many long years after the war until, that is, I read the Upanishads. A chance discovery of this ancient philosophical Sanskrit text restored my trust in humanity and eventually cleared my confused and wounded mind.

I am writing these notes in the spring of 2013. However, my interest in Advaita began at the age of twenty-two in 1958 while studying political science in Paris. Ever since then, Advaita has been my private passion. I rarely felt the need or the desire to share this personal interest with others. That is, until six months ago, to my surprise, I began writing my own interpretation of this unusual and uncommon subject. I assume that the reason for this writing is to share it with others.

But I also have another personal reason. What I have written is a book such as I would have loved to read myself. I noticed that while most literature on Advaita frequently mentions that to gain Self-Realization, an in-depth inquiry into the notion of "Self" is necessary, none of these texts explain how it is done. It occurred to me that I should write my own version of what happens during the process of what is labeled in Advaita as the "I-inquiry." From my perspective, that is the purpose of writing HOLY VOID.

I abandoned the study of political science soon after reading about Advaita in the Upanishads. And at the beginning of 1960, I enrolled at the University of Madras in India and studied Advaita philosophy there for five years with Professor T. M. P. Mahadevan. His PhD research was in Advaita philosophy; his knowledge suited well my interest in this classic Upanishadic epistemological tradition. Although I did receive a University of Madras master of arts degree in philosophy, my interest of studying Advaita was motivated by my personal spiritual need and not by academic reasons.

After landing in Bombay in January 1960, I was greeted by a sweet and colorful individual, with whom I was in correspondence from Paris, dressed like Mahatma Gandhi, with an exotic local name of Bharatananda, otherwise known as Maurice Frydman. A decade later he became known as the discoverer of Nisargadatta, whose Advaita teachings were popularized through his book I Am That. Immediately, after a warm greeting, he spontaneously assumed the role of my mentor; this role stayed with him for the rest of his life, to my delight.

A week later, I landed in Madras, a hot and humid city. I was greeted by a frail lady, wrapped from head to toe in a colorful sari, with prominently displayed Hindu red kumkum on her forehead, wearing dark sunglasses covering most of her face. She introduced herself with her Hindu name as Umadevi, a known Polish author on Theosophy by the name of Wanda Dynowska, a devout convert to Hinduism since the 1930s. She is the one who sent me my first book I read on Advaita by Ramana Maharshi of Arunachala.

Decades later, I realized that the study of Ramana Maharshi's spirituality had a crucial and unmatched influence on my understanding of Classic Advaita. Although most of what has been published about him was redacted into verbal and conceptual language, if one is prepared to hunt for nondual and nonverbal meaning, it is available there too. My book, *HOLY VOID*, is essentially an attempt to demonstrate the validity of Ramana Maharshi's statement "to think is not your real nature."

Bharatananda and Umadevi, both Theosophists who lived in India since the early 1930s, were instrumental in introducing me to various spiritual groups and gurus. I will mention two such memorable introductions. Through Bharatananda I had the opportunity to meet Jiddu Krishnamurti, whose teachings became a source of inspiration and numerous emotional and mental realizations. Through Umadevi I met N. Sri Ram, president of the Theosophical Society, whose succinct answers to my questions triggered many instantaneous verbal enlightenments.

My interest in spirituality propelled me for many years to visit numerous teachers. Some of them became known in the West years later, like His Holiness the Dalai Lama of Tibet, who had recently escaped Chinese invasion, and Maharishi Mahesh in Rishikesh, creator of Transcendental Meditation. Also, I visited the Aurobindo spiritual center in Pondicherry. I continued, almost obsessively, visiting gurus not only in India but also later in the West. For example,

I will mention two more widely known in academic circles: Wei Wu Wei (Terence James Stannus Gray), a writer on nonconceptual Tao philosophy with whom I had a meeting in Switzerland, and Alan Watts, whose talks on Zen I attended in California.

Somewhere in spiritual writings I read that the guru is the one who instructs you about Mahavakyas (Great Statements). If so, in my life then, this distinction goes to my professor of philosophy at the University of Madras, T. M. P. Mahadevan. Today, after more than five decades, I still remember as if it was yesterday how during the reading of the fifth chapter entitled "Mahavakya Viveka of Vidyaranya's Panchadasi," a fourteenth-century Advaita classic, Professor Mahadevan explained the meaning of *Prajnanam Brahma*, the meaning of *Aham Brahma Asmi*, the meaning of *Tat Tvam Asi*, and the meaning of *Ayam Atma Brahma*. Which means, respectively: *Consciousness Is the Absolute*, and *I Am the Absolute*, and *That You Are*, and *The Self Is the Absolute*. These Great Statements, which encapsulate the essence of Advaita realization, have reverberated in my intellect ever since.

After five years of numerous contacts with many gurus of India and after much study with Professor Mahadevan, and with my mind overflowing with conceptual knowledge about Advaita, I returned to France, and shortly after, I found myself in the middle of the LSD craze in American university circles. Professor Timothy Leary was advocating a new psychedelic spiritual revolution based on the chemistry of the mind—or rather the brain. Along with my interest in this new movement, I continued my obsessive hunt of spiritual gurus regularly invading the American spiritual market.

In 1969 I came across a unique spiritual teaching called Sant Mat, which although originally from India was also known in many Western countries. The initiation, by Master Charan Singh, into this intense, rigorous, and effective metaphysical meditation method kept me busy for almost Two decades. During this time my obsessive urge to seek gurus subsided and my mind became alert and focused. I felt privileged and humbled to be initiated into such a noble spiritual path. Also, I was spared the psychedelic confusion prevalent in those days.

In the second half of the 1980s, my extensive period of Sant Mat meditation culminated in a vigorous, intense, and renewed longing for my original interest in Advaita, or nondual consciousness. I became impatient with my progress and tired of the lack of spiritual achievement at this point in my life.

All over again, my old urge to hunt gurus returned intact. I wanted to be sure that I did not miss something from a variety of gurus who continuously flocked to Hollywood where I lived and worked in the motion picture industry. Hollywood is not only the mecca for cinematographic arts but also for gurus and for countless varieties of religious and secular creeds ranging from the believers in Mazdaism of ancient Zoroastrians to practitioners of the futuristic Scientology of L. Ron Hubbard. Undeniably, time spent in the company of spiritual teachers has always been and still was the most rewarding experience. Yet this time my spiritual thirst would not and could not be quenched by conceptual instructions offered by most gurus. My conditioned mind had no more room for additional conditioning. I already had decades of such exposure, and I felt that I had outgrown the need for more intellectual explanations and sensational temporary mental enlightenments easily available to eager spiritual seekers like myself.

My three-decades-long seeking ended in severe disappointment with the results. My desperate spiritual search came to a head. Deep in my being, a spontaneous and intense questioning began: Where are the promises of the Upanishads I read in my youth, that by knowing the Self everything else becomes known? Why is it that most gurus do not tell me clearly how to know my Higher Self? Why are so many lengthy books and hours of lectures and discussions filled with exotic explanations? Why so many concepts? Why so many words? Is our consciousness so complex? Why am I asking? Who is asking?

It is when my attention turned not against but away from gurus, not against but away from the influences of outside conditioning, that I realized this entire spiritual drama, including being disappointed by the lack of spiritual progress, was taking place not in me but in my own mind—better yet, not in my own mind but in my preconditioned and culturally acquired, from outside, *collective* mind, which resides and functions inside of my own consciousness. This seemingly insignificant and silent shift of my attention, from *outside to inside*, had, for the first time, also silently triggered a spontaneous inquiry into my inner being. I asked: "Who or what is this consciousness I feel within my inner self from birth?" This inquiry culminated in, also silent, awareness—which I can describe in poetic terms as a silent expanse of divine everlasting presence—that has remained with me since. And yet this silent divine presence surprised me with its simplicity.

At first, I could not accept that this inner divine expanse of consciousness is the one I had all along since my birth. Also, I could not categorize it as "experience," which starts and ends, because it has always been there, whereas experience is confined and limited to a specific event. This silent acknowledgment of my nature is not an event and not a verbal experience. Also, it is nothing new and nothing extraordinary. The ordinary nature of this realization took several years to be fully appreciated.

I am still unable to adequately define or describe this divine everlasting presence; I suppose that it is so because its nature is nonverbal. I can only acknowledge that my attention stays naturally and preferably inside this nonverbal everlasting presence instead of running out in pursuit of restless seeking. But since it is not a conceptual condition, my mind cannot grasp it or know it; it has zero thought. Therefore, I like to label it as a *holy void*.

It is much easier to describe the effect this realization has on the verbal or mental part of my awareness. For example, though my thinking mind functions smoothly in utilitarian matters, I clearly realize that this mind has lost its former importance and is no longer vested with the power to supply spiritual knowledge. I am aware now how thinking is foreign or external to my innate nonverbal consciousness or that thinking is *not* my consciousness but is *in* my consciousness. I have a definite feeling of being free from the oppressive authority of thought. This freedom is also accompanied with a feeling of surprise at how simple, obvious, and natural this realization is. Instead of being, as I thought before, supernatural, this realization is supremely natural. And above all, instead of being a fantastic new experience, it is void of any recognizable sensations commonly known as experiences. My existence or my is-ness or my being-ness is silent, without mental sensations; it is simply a realization of what I already am.

Ever since then, my urge to seek any spiritual philosophy different from my original interest in Advaita has silently and utterly faded away. Now, it is this nonverbal everlasting presence that succeeds to hold my silent attention within my innate holy void.

INTRODUCTION

Albert Einstein is quoted as saying, "Science, measured against reality, is primitive and childlike—and yet it is the most precious thing we have." Agreed. However, this "precious," "primitive" and "childlike" science, an important building block of civilization, exists because our consciousness makes science possible. We are able to learn how to use fire, control nuclear fusion, create religions, and establish efficient sociopolitical systems because of our consciousness.

Consciousness has been discussed throughout history. In ancient Vedas consciousness is identified as being *without name and form*. This means that consciousness is nonverbal. In this book I explain the significance of being aware of nonverbal consciousness.

CONSCIOUSNESS

Thinking and Consciousness

We know that the mind is composed of thoughts. We may not re-alize that every thought and word, without exception, has entered our mind from the outside world of our civilization. Thoughts do not originate from our consciousness. We progressively acquire thoughts from the agelong accumulation of verbal information present in our collective cultural environment. These acquired thoughts are stored in our consciousness. They are about survival needs such as practical know-how, scientific knowledge, sociopo-litical principles, aesthetic norms, and moral codes. And thoughts are also the fabric of indoctrination into religious teachings, archaic mythological beliefs, misinformation, superstitions, prejudices, and thoughts about what and who I am. This cultural verbal condition-ing, which continues during our entire life, establishes a complex utilitarian instrument that is our amazing thinking mind.

If thoughts are stored in our consciousness but are not consciousness, then what is our consciousness? It follows that our consciousness must be present in us before the acquisition of thoughts. And indeed, it is so. We are born with consciousness but without thoughts.

Here is the point. Thinking appears to be consciousness, but thinking is a culturally acquired mental function. Our thinking mind is a utilitarian tool that creates new combinations of ideas needed for our survival in a diverse phenomenal world. Although thinking resides in consciousness, thinking itself is not our innate consciousness.

The consciousness we have at birth is nonverbal, meaning not made of words. Also, this consciousness is universal. This universality means there is no other consciousness. Referred to as *spirit*, this innate universal nonverbal consciousness is the source of intelligence, wisdom, and well-being. Our culturally acquired thinking mind and our civilization depend on our consciousness.

When we observe our acquired thinking, we realize that thoughts give us reliable information needed for survival. We do not realize that what we call our objective reliable information is a subjective belief that it is objective. Verbal information is subjective because it depends on the thinking mind, an arsenal of acquired fragments of information, called *concepts*, unique to each one of us. The mind is well suited to deal with acquired verbal constructs but not with our nonverbal innate consciousness.

So thinking is our culturally acquired commodity in consciousness, but consciousness itself is not acquired. It is present in us from birth and is not composed of thoughts. And when we become aware of our innate nonverbal consciousness, we become aware of our spirituality.

Spirituality

Spirituality does not depend on our culturally acquired thoughts and cannot be adequately explained or defined verbally. Spirituality is neither a mental concept nor a belief. Our acquired thinking mind is an excellent instrument for dealing with practical needs in the phenomenal world, but the thinking mind is not equipped to deal with our innate consciousness. Our consciousness is not of the mind.

So what is spirituality? Spirituality is awareness of the consciousness we are at birth; we are spiritual nonverbal consciousness.

Nonverbal Consciousness

How are we aware of nonverbal consciousness? To know that *I am* is the direct awareness of our nonverbal consciousness, not of our thinking mind. Also, our attention is nonverbal consciousness. Although this attention can be given to our thinking, the attention itself is not a thought. Then, after waking up from deep sleep, we remember the absence of thinking while we were asleep. This act of remembering indicates that there was an awareness of nonverbal consciousness.

When we think that our thoughts are consciousness, we remain unaware that our existence is known without the participation of our thoughts. Even in the field of leading thinkers and philosophers, this awareness is absent. For example, René Descartes, known as one of the fathers of modern philosophy, said, "I think, therefore I am." This is a classic example of how our thinking dominates what we know. We fail to notice that we are conscious without the presence of thinking. I am aware of my being without any thought. This awareness is nonverbal consciousness.

So this is what we know. I am conscious that I exist without having to think about it. I exist in deep sleep where there is no thinking. I cannot think myself out of existence, meaning I cannot deny that I am. Awareness of all this is due to my innate nonverbal consciousness.

It is noteworthy to point out that in philosophy the statement *I am* is understood as a judgment based on thought-centered consciousness. The *I am* is a concept that comes into view after it goes through the process of thinking. It is an indirect perception. Whereas when the *I am* is understood as a label that represents nonconceptual, thought-absent consciousness, present before and in spite of thinking, then the *I am* is not a thought but a direct nonverbal awareness of existence.

The inability to distinguish between thinking and our innate nonverbal awareness is deeply rooted in most of us. This leads to absurd notions such as I think, therefore I exist. It is obvious that we must exist before we can think, not the other way around.

Being aware nonverbally and thinking are different from each other. Noticing this difference is essential in understanding consciousness. Not noticing this leads to confusion and misunderstanding.

Our thinking changes constantly. Our nonverbal consciousness is permanent; we know it as our always present attention. It is not thinking but our innate nonverbal consciousness that is the foundation of our awareness. I am aware of my existence nonverbally.

The Inquiry

Since we usually consider our thinking mind as our consciousness and the source of valid spiritual knowledge, we need to disentangle ourselves from this misconception. The way this is achieved is using inquiry.

If this misconception persists, the intellectual question who am I is the right inquiry in the quest for self-knowledge. However, once this error becomes evident, the question becomes redundant and is understood to be an absurd intellectual question. The idea of knowledge about the self is bordering on the absurd since we would need a second self to know about the first self. Obviously there is one self, not two. In spite of this apparent absurdity, the inquiry into who I am will show us that the belief that thinking is our consciousness is a cultural misconception.

Here is what occurs during the *who am I* question. This question is initiated by the mind asking the mind to find the origin of the *I*, which is also a notion of the mind. We can say the mind is faced with a dilemma of its own making. The mind is not equipped to deal with questions about itself. As a result, the mind goes blank while the permanent presence of our nonverbal consciousness is exposed and noticed by our attention. This is how the mind is circumvented. Our attention stays with our nonverbal awareness. Since this nonverbal awareness is not a concept, the mind perceives it as a mental void. However, there is someone who is conscious of this void. This someone is our solid and well-established nonverbal consciousness, also called *attention* or *nonverbal I*.

Through inquiry into *who am I*, we come upon the presence of verbally undefined awareness, the mental void. It is the same nonverbal experience of consciousness that occurs in deep sleep as well as in the nonverbal awareness of our attention and in the nonverbal awareness of the *I am*.

Acknowledgment of the verbal void or nothingness does not ordinarily occur because we habitually focus our attention on thinking and speaking. For those who may feel uncomfortable about the idea of void or nothingness, we need to stress that these notions refer to the absence of words or thoughts during inquiry. There is no absolute void or nothingness, and it is not even possible to conceive of it. Obviously, in matters of utilitarian and scientific endeavors, thoughts are essential. On the other hand, the absence of thought that occurs during inquiry is experienced as a solid presence of innate awareness, labeled *nonverbal consciousness.*

A typical popular spiritual question among seekers is how do I become enlightened. If we ask who is this *I* that wants enlightenment, the inquiry takes us straight to the mental void, which is, as we know now, our nonverbal consciousness. Meanwhile, during this process, the question itself has disappeared. This clearly demonstrates that inquiry is a means of becoming aware of nonverbal consciousness. Desires disappear when they are fulfilled. Does it mean that the desire for enlightenment is fulfilled? Can the act of inquiry accomplish such a feat? If those thoughts dissolve into nonverbal consciousness, is that nonverbal consciousness enlightenment? The answer is yes. Awareness of our nonverbal consciousness is enlightenment.

Through inquiry, thoughts disappear into a mental void. This tells us that thinking is not the permanent consciousness with which we are born. This tells us that thinking is not consciousness. With awareness of our innate nonverbal consciousness, we realize that words have a fleeting impact on us. Verbal wants are temporary. On the other hand, our innate nonverbal consciousness is solid and permanent. It is the core of our being.

The essence of attention is nonverbal consciousness, but our deeply ingrained cultural habit of relying primarily on thought-centered cognition is overpowering. Now we understand that nonverbal consciousness is the *I* of the thinker. So essentially, what it takes is to shift our attention from thinking to the thinker. This task is accomplished effectively through inquiry. The **who am I** inquiry is a method that uses acquired mental meanings to expose the ever-present nonverbal consciousness. The inquiry is an effective means to free us from the overpowering hold that thinking has on our consciousness.

Thoughts Versus Consciousness

Thoughts are not the same as consciousness. Thoughts are cultur-ally acquired utilitarian tools for survival needs. Consciousness is present at birth.

Thoughts are observable temporary components of our mind. Thoughts are dependent on our cultural exposure and change accordingly. Thoughts are ideas, fragmented bits and pieces of verbal information about what we can call the undifferentiated existence that is our world. Consciousness does not come about. Consciousness is always present and is not observable.

Acquired mental skills differ between individuals as we adapt to specific languages and cultural conditions, but we are all born with nonverbal consciousness.

Nonverbal consciousness is always present, overwhelmingly still and devoid of thoughts. Consciousness exists without thinking. Thinking cannot exist without consciousness. Knowing this, the habit of believing that thinking is our consciousness stops.

So then what is our consciousness? Can we investigate it? Can we know it like we know thoughts? How can we? Consciousness is not an object that can be examined. Consciousness is that which makes the investigating and the knowing possible.

We live immersed in consciousness. Consciousness is the quintessence of existence. The phenomenal world is a reflection of consciousness. If consciousness is present in us at birth and the world is undifferentiated, then consciousness is present in every creature and in every particle.

We are born with undifferentiated consciousness. Thinking, an acquired utensil for survival, resides in undifferentiated consciousness.

Nonverbal Self

Being aware of our nonverbal consciousness is important. In that nonverbal stillness there is no confusion, misunderstanding, or unhappiness. We know this from the mute comfort of deep sleep, where thoughts are absent, and from the silent awareness of the *I am* that does not need thinking. We know it from inquiry into the origin of *I* when our questioning leads to awareness of nonverbal consciousness.

Does this mean that thinking is a source of trouble? If thinking is assumed to be consciousness, then it can be. This assumption creates an unreal sense of mental self-importance, an inflated ego. If our attention stays in nonverbal consciousness, the ego does not inflate, and our thinking deals efficiently with daily life.

How can we keep our attention in nonverbal consciousness? We are always in this consciousness. We, you and I, are consciousness itself. To be aware of this is the same as our innate awareness that we exist. Consciousness is present in our awareness of *I am*. It is present when we sleep, dream, daydream, imagine, or think. And when we trace our thinking to its source through inquiry, consciousness is there too. Also, our mind is a phenomenal expression of this consciousness.

When we know this, we realize that the core of nonverbal

consciousness is our attention. This is the moment of realization that the permanent and silent nonverbal consciousness as our attention is our ever-present nonverbal self. This is the answer to our question *who am I*.

This knowledge is the culmination of the inquiry. Additional inquiry becomes unnecessary. Our attention shifts from fragmented thought-centered cognition to the solid awareness of our nonverbal consciousness called the nonverbal self. Our nonverbal self can be described as what it is not, not what it is. If it could be described verbally, it would be a concept in our thinking mind. Our nonverbal self comes in full view, not as a concept but as presence.

This realization brings an end to the need for mental spiritual knowing. What remains is nonpersonal attention. I refer to this realization as *holy void* and *zero-thought-consciousness*.

Attention

The awareness of this already existing attention as consciousness is the culmination of our spiritual quest. Now we realize that consciousness is not our culturally acquired thoughts. This familiar and ordinary attention is the original consciousness.

Nonverbal Realization

The inquiry leads to the realization that we are the nonverbal self, and this creates new mental paradigms of understanding. Now we realize that our consciousness is not our thinking but our innate nonverbal attention. We know that thinking is acquired to meet the challenges of survival. Thinking is a utilitarian tool, not a source of spiritual knowledge. This realization removes the cause for mental spiritual seeking. No longer subjugated by thoughts, our attention shifts. The usual outward pursuit of mental spiritual seeking stops. Our attention stays in nonverbal innate consciousness. To be aware nonverbally is to be who I am. I am consciousness.

INTERLUDE I

Conceptual understanding is not the same as the awareness of non-verbal presence. If we believe that conceptual understanding is our consciousness, we remain in a state of mental delusion, unaware of the presence of our innate nonverbal consciousness. Thinking is an instrument for survival, and our nonverbal consciousness is our spiritual awareness. The reason we do the inquiry is to notice the presence of nonverbal consciousness.

Conceptual truth does not matter in nonverbal realization. Our culturally acquired utilitarian thinking mind creates the need for verbal truth. The acquired verbal spiritual truth, including the acquired verbal truth of this book, is a mental fiction and need not be remembered. Verbal explanations of truth keep us locked in a labyrinth of culturally acquired thoughts. Nonverbal truth is a pragmatic realization.

We are unknown to our own thoughts. The mind is not capable of answering the *who am I* question. This means that the mind cannot know our nonverbal *I*. The thinking mind is capable of knowing acquired ideas. The awareness of our nonverbal self is a realization within our innate nonverbal consciousness, not a mental knowing. The awareness that the self is nonverbal stays with us for the rest of our life.

We do not advocate any new mental truth but recommend the method of inquiry to reveal the already existing nonverbal consciousness, referred to as our attention and also as nonverbal self.

We remain conscious without thoughts; this means that we are nonverbal consciousness. Culturally acquired thoughts are peripheral to what we are by birth. This realization frees us from the quagmire of beliefs that are culturally acquired superstitions.

REFLECTIONS

The Way of Inquiry

One way to access awareness of our nonverbal consciousness is through inquiry into the origin of the *I*. In this approach, the entire effort is concentrated on what happens during the process leading to nonverbal realization. After that, inquiry is not needed.

Essentially, the inquirer conducts an inquiry into themselves. The main purpose is to demonstrate the presence of nonverbal consciousness within the inquirer. This leads to the awareness that our ordinary attention is the nonverbal self.

We arrive at this nonverbal awareness by means of the mind. Our fragmenting mind no longer assumes the leading role of consciousness. Instead, we use it as an instrument to locate our nonverbal consciousness.

The main obstacle in describing anything nonverbal is that language uses words. There are no words for nonverbal awareness.

However, we can state what it is not and use paradoxical expressions such as nonpersonal selfhood. Consequently, the mind has nothing conceptual to grasp, and we come to realize that this nothing is the something we seek, the innate nonverbal consciousness.

The absence of suitable mental definitions for nonverbal awareness leads to silence. Such is the realm of spiritual nonverbal awareness. That is why many spiritual traditions speak of teaching through silence. Silence is the permanent condition of consciousness itself. Consciousness has no sound, no color, no shape, no dimension. Time does not touch it. It is not young and does not get old.

To reach consciousness through silence is ideal, and it does happen at moments of realization. These silent moments of realization can be reached using common language that points us in the direction of nonverbal attention.

Traditional philosophical thinking is confined to the conceptual realm and does not offer any possible means to step out of it. Conceptual definitions do not give us awareness of our innate nonverbal consciousness. Concepts are helpful for inquiry, but they are not ends in themselves.

Confinement within the realm of conceptual thinking is unknowingly propagated by spiritual writings. Our mind can imagine nonverbal realizations in the form of conceptual truths. There is a profusion of conceptual descriptions explaining the wonders of nonverbal spiritual enlightenment. Although descriptions of enlightenment are enticing, they can be a source of intellectual confinement. We forget that nonverbal awareness can be realized empirically as presence in our attention. It cannot and need not be described with concepts.

A civilization that decides about our philosophical, spiritual, religious, secular, and mythological beliefs confines us to the intellectual realm of concepts. Conceptual convictions in the form of common beliefs are acquired from our cultural conditioning. We are willing participants in the common beliefs that confine us. Cultural common beliefs give us tribal security, a form of group hypnosis.

Another type of mental confinement is to reject everything not conceptual and explained by reason or to reject everything reasonable because it is not spiritual. In both cases we are reacting from the limited realm of thinking. Between these two extremes, the fragmenting mind keeps reacting all day long prompted by cultural conditioning. The mind latches on to a familiar set of convictions to be sure it has a defined role to play. This is the most common conceptual confinement there is.

The feeling within us that something is missing and the psychological urge to become someone in the future are due to overreliance on thought-centered conceptual confinement. No amount of institutionalized spiritual promises can ever satisfy a restless mind until we find the awareness of nonverbal consciousness. When we no longer rely on thinking for spiritual knowledge, we free our attention to act from nonverbal consciousness instead of words.

The way of inquiry offers a means to be aware of nonverbal consciousness. How? By demonstrating it. This demonstration consists of being able to acknowledge the nonverbal void, the nothingness that occurs during inquiry. Acknowledging the presence of nonverbal consciousness in the form of verbal nothingness, which is zero-thought-consciousness, leads to awareness of the permanent presence of this ordinary nonverbal attention, the nonverbal self.

Mental Void

For some of us, the notions of mental void as our solid nonverbal consciousness and empty mind as freedom from thoughts are pure fantasy. For others, the terms *void* and *zero-thought-consciousness* are nihilistic. And for those who follow the literal interpretation of scriptures, these terms are a threat to the comfort found in verbal meanings.

The above is true for those who are convinced that spiritual knowledge comes from verbal, conceptual definitions. To step out of mental confinement is not supported in a civilization dominated by verbal injunctions that govern our sociopolitical and spiritual lives. Our societies are ruled primarily by ideas, and our ideas have become our realities.

What is reality? Obviously, reality is more than ideas. Ideas are part of that reality. This small distinction has big implications. It is the opening for investigation. Inquiry inevitably leads to the realization that our lives are complex and cannot easily be confined to words.

Words have multiple meanings and are often the cause for lack of clarity. What happens to those of us who rely on words alone? Deep down within we detect a distrust of the information derived from words. We carry this private conviction from early childhood after being confronted time and time again with a discrepancy between what we hear being said and what we experience and see. As adults we become cynical and suspicious, or, like the majority, we continue to ignore our distrust and pretend that words represent reality. However, ignoring this distrust has long-term consequences. Unknowingly we develop the skillful art of compensation by dramatizing our verbal convictions to make them more believable to others and ourselves. Thus, from ornate platforms and pulpits we proclaim lofty verbal truths. But across the waters and borders, others proclaim verbal truths that may be contrary to ours. Is this fertile ground for conflict?

Words do not and cannot give us spiritual realization. Words are limited instruments to convey phenomenal events. The wealth of spiritual meaning is to be found not in conceptual meanings but in their absence. The inexplicable divine is found in the mental void.

Illusion

That the world is an illusion is a common concept in Eastern philosophy. This concept has been discussed in Western philosophy, but mostly in the past. Recently this concept became an accepted proposition in quantum physics under the label of uncertainty. Some may challenge this analogy, but it is a question of semantics. Both illusion and uncertainty mean that what we see is not necessarily what is.

What is reality? Quantum physicists say the conditions of perception determine the phenomena. So each time the conditions of perception change, a different phenomenal reality is perceived. Whereas, with awareness of nonverbal consciousness, we do not know what reality is, not because of the changing conditions of perception but because the notion of *reality* is a concept that stands for something made up by our fragmenting mind.

If the existence of the world is perceived as a concept, the way the mind perceives it, then this type of perception is an illusion. The notion of illusion applies to the conceptual way of understanding our world, not to the world itself. With awareness of nonverbal consciousness, the world, including us, is undifferentiated universal consciousness.

Solipsism

Solipsism is a philosophical subjective idealism in which the world is an idea created by the self. The world does not exist in the way the self does. In solipsism the single reality proven to exist is the self, not the world. Although with awareness of nonverbal consciousness we understand that perceptions of the world are subjective and objective perceptions are a subjective belief that they are objective, we do not come to the same conclusion as solipsism. Solipsism deals with the existence of the world on the level of conceptual fragmented thinking, and we explain the existence of the world from the standpoint of nonverbal awareness. We consider the self as nonverbal presence that cannot be denied, and we agree with solipsism that we know the world as an idea. But ideas are conceptual forms of consciousness, and consciousness is existence. We do not deny the existence of the world. The world exists as the same consciousness that is present in the self. There is nothing but existence. It is not possible to conceive of nonexistence. We cannot deny our own existence or the existence of the world. The world and the self are undifferentiated existence.

Gnosticism

An archaeological discovery in Upper Egypt in 1945, Gnostic writings are strikingly similar in content to Advaita in the Upanishads, Buddhist texts, and what we say about the awareness of nonverbal consciousness. For example, Gnostics say that those who do not know their own self know nothing, but those who know their own self have knowledge about the depth of things.

The method of achieving this knowledge through self-inquiry is also very similar. Gnostic texts clearly point to the *I*. For example, who is within you who says my mind, my thoughts, my body? Gnosticism maintains that the ultimate spiritual insight is not gained through intellectual knowledge but through *gnosis*, which is nonverbal empirical realization.

These many similarities lead some historians to suggest Gnostics were influenced by ideas from India. It can also be argued that what Gnosticism says is so basic to human life, it can take place independently anywhere without the need for any influence.

Gnostics did not deify Christ but considered him a revered spiritual guide. Their understanding of consciousness is not limited to purely religious goals.

Mythology and Poetry

In the pursuit of spirituality, mythology and poetry are two opposite poles in the spectrum of mental activity. On the mythological side is the literal understanding of our invented religious and sociopolitical beliefs, and on the poetry side are literary descriptions of nonverbal spiritual experiences. Between these two there is rationality and common sense.

Myths prevalent in most organized world religions stem from an archaic, unproven, and never questioned belief that there is a separation between humans and God. This belief is supported by the conviction that there is an outside entity called God never seen anywhere other than in our imagination. These mythological dogmas are the starting point of myriad unsubstantiated creeds. Similarly, our sociopolitical doctrines, such as anarchy, government rule, socialism, capitalism, and communism, are in essence imaginary beliefs, similar to religious myths.

In spite of being naïve, religious and sociopolitical myths have cultural appeal. Organized religions use them to promote moral values, and politicians use them to promote social order. The same mythical beliefs lead to social disorder, fanatic behavior, and divisions among people.

In the poetry about nonverbal spiritual experiences, God is understood as our innate consciousness, not as an outside entity. This poetry is a play of complex conceptual meanings that attempt to peer into the nonverbal realm of our innate divine consciousness. The frequent use of paradox is a firm indication of poetic attempts to describe this something that is verbally indefinable, which we label nonverbal consciousness. The similarity is evident.

Being aware of this wide range of mental capabilities teaches us to be cautious about blindly accepting our mythological beliefs and to not underestimate the spiritual value of poetic reports of the nonverbal divine presence within us.

The Mind

If the mind is not consciousness, then what is its role?

Divide and rule. This political and military tactic shows us how our mind functions. The mind has been perfectly honed through the millennia to be an unceasing dividing instrument. Our thinking mind can be a constructive and destructive power. We will focus on how this powerful ruler can be a cooperative and helpful agent.

We are born without thoughts. We are also born with the ability to have a mind, but its contents are acquired from the outside world. Thoughts, in the shape of words, originate from the civilization we belong to. We inherit our mental culture, whether it is rational or mythological, from outside. This is the conditioning of the mind. This process lasts throughout our entire life. This cultural training is not part of our innate nonverbal consciousness. It takes place in our mind alone. Thinking is an acquired survival tool based on utilitarian beliefs.

Although thinking is not our innate consciousness, most of us believe that it is. We are convinced that thinking is consciousness. This misconception causes spiritual confusion.

The mind is useful to discern between distinct types of ideas. Ideas based on intangible elements, such as resurrection, ascension, reincarnation, karma, heaven, hell, walking on water, supernatural appearances, and the like, are constructs of our imagination. They may be useful as entertainment or mental exercises. However, if taken as realities, they are misleading. Ideas based on tangible elements, such as how to travel to the moon, how to clean the environment, what is the proper diet for healthy living, ideas about cooperation between different social groups, and the like, are related to practical survival needs. The discerning mind is essential for our survival.

The mind not understood as a useful discerning agent can be an unruly foe. It assumes the role of consciousness and takes over the affairs of our world. The mind works well to formulate appropriate identification labels but not to know reality. It is a navigation tool in this multifarious world. This is the role of our thinking utilitarian mind. The mind cannot and will not give us a comprehensive understanding of our world.

Imagination is useful when understood as imagination. The same imagination, however, can be a source of nefarious behavior when its contents are taken as absolute realities instead of conceptual fantasies. If conceptual fantasies become political or religious beliefs, they are misleading and can result in social division and conflict.

What the mind does well is to give us a comprehensive under-standing of words. Our knowledge is based on a clear understanding of concepts, but in nonverbal consciousness concepts are not reality. They are attempts to describe phenomena, and that description changes with each new understanding.

Our mind can assume an infinite number of convincing roles and functions. Once understood, we can use it as a tool instead of being used by it.

Understanding the mind is helped by using the method of inquiry. Through inquiry we use our ability to convert our mental content into nonverbal consciousness. By asking the question who wants to understand the mind, we will come upon a mental void. Do not dismiss this void as nothing. This void is our nonverbal consciousness. How? Note carefully. Someone must be there to be aware of this void. That someone is our nonverbal innate consciousness, the nonverbal self. That is how we know the mind cannot function without this consciousness. The mind is not an independent entity and is not in charge of consciousness. The mind is dependent on our innate nonverbal consciousness, our spirit.

Why is it important to know that the mind is dependent? Knowing this changes our perception. Once aware of our nonverbal consciousness, we no longer merely view the world as divided into entities separated from each other by our fragmenting mind. We realize that the world is undifferentiated existence.

The point is that the mind is an acquired verbal tool in consciousness, a conceptual fiction created by our fragmented thoughts. The mind is not consciousness. I am consciousness.

INTERLUDE II

It is easy to fall for conceptual explanations of spirituality as if they were spiritual realizations. Culturally acquired thinking can be an impediment to spiritual awareness. At the same time, concepts can be used in inquiry as hypothetical working assumptions to reveal our innate identity as nonverbal consciousness. And concepts perform appropriate functions as useful instruments for mental explanations and practical knowledge.

Spiritual realization, however, is not based on conceptual knowledge. The mind is alien to the nonverbal consciousness that we have at birth. This nonverbal consciousness is our source of wisdom. With this realization, the expectation to know spirituality with our mental ability stops. Awareness of our innate nonverbal consciousness frees us from the tyranny of thought.

CONVERSATIONS

After finishing my graduate work in the philosophy department at the University of Madras, I spoke in Paris, Brussels, New York, and Los Angeles at gatherings of people interested in Advaita. This was made possible through introductions from my mentors Maurice Frydman (a.k.a. Bharatananda) and Wanda Dynowska (a.k.a. Umadevi). This next part, titled "Conversations," contains the most common recurring themes that emerged during the discussions that followed my presentations.

Questions and Answers

You say we are born with nonverbal consciousness without thoughts, which you call zero-thought-consciousness, mental void, and holy void. What happens when we realize that we are born without thoughts?
When we realize this, we function with awareness of our innate spiritual nonverbal consciousness.

And if we do not realize this?

If we do not, our attention stays with thoughts, and we function with secular and religious beliefs acquired from our civilization.

———

I am afraid of emptiness and nothingness. I am afraid I will disappear in the void. Why emphasize these ideas? I would expect true spirituality to be positive.

We are not talking about absolute void or nothingness. There is no such thing. Emptiness, nothingness, and void refer to an absence of thinking. This absence allows us to notice our nonverbal consciousness that is ordinarily obstructed by our thoughts. Fear of these concepts indicates you are convinced that thinking is your consciousness. This is what you need to examine first.

I can't see how thinking is not my consciousness.

It appears this way until you uncover that you have awareness without the presence of thinking.

I always have thoughts. I always think.

You do not need to think to be aware that you exist. With this awareness, you have an enormous amount of information that you did not get from thinking. For example, you can see light, hear sounds, smell flowers, feel temperature, walk, talk, know up and down, and so on. There is no reason to be afraid of the absence of thought. If we inquire into our consciousness, we find that most of our daily activities are spent in nonverbal awareness, empty of thoughts. Thinking is a small part of it.

How do I become aware of my nonverbal consciousness?

Watch your attention. The attention itself is nonverbal. When you watch it, you realize that you see your own innate consciousness, which is void of thoughts.

—

Why is it that what you are talking about is so difficult to understand?

How to be aware of nonverbal consciousness is not easy to understand. Our cultural conditioning relies on verbal information. Thinking is the source of our survival know-how and spiritual truth. Questioning our cultural conditioning is a prerequisite to self-knowledge. For most people, however, questioning this conditioning is a threat to mental and emotional security. It requires a certain maturity of mind to understand nonverbal consciousness without feeling that our safety is in jeopardy.

What does it mean to have maturity of mind?

Mental maturity is when we no longer expect to get spiritual knowledge from verbal information.

What is the advantage of being aware of our nonverbal consciousness?

Awareness of our nonverbal consciousness frees us from relying on thinking for spiritual guidance. And as the burden of mental beliefs is lifted, our thinking mind is free to function efficiently as the overseer of our practical survival needs. Nonverbal consciousness is divine consciousness. Awareness of nonverbal consciousness is enlightenment.

—

Why do you define spirituality as awareness of our nonverbal consciousness?

What is spirituality? Spirituality is awareness of the consciousness we are at birth. That consciousness is nonverbal. Many spiritual disciplines describe spiritual realization as the awareness of our innate divine nonverbal consciousness.

How is nonverbal consciousness described in traditional spiritual writings?

I will give a few examples from the ancient writings called the Vedas. One example is self-luminous directly experienced consciousness. Then there is consciousness that transcends the body, senses, and mind. Another example is consciousness without change or modification. The most common definition is consciousness without name or form. There are more, but these are a few major ones that come to mind.

———

I heard you mention holy void. What is it? Where is it? Can anyone experience it? Can I experience it? You say it's ever-present, ordinary, and obvious. I do not see it.

Holy void is a label for the divine consciousness that we are at birth. We know this ever-present consciousness as our attention.

How?

Do you mean that you are not aware of your attention?

I am aware of my attention. But how does one—or how can I experience this holy void you talk about?

You probably expect it to appear like a blazing light in a bush. Cultural mythology conditions our mind to expect miracles that appear as fantastic events in the outside world. We do not realize that our existence is a miracle, and the blazing light is our ordinary consciousness. For instance, when you close your eyes and put your ordinary attention on your attention, you are aware of your own usual consciousness. This consciousness is not a thought or concept or a myth. It is a presence. This innate divine consciousness is void of any thinking and void of any meaning conjured by our mind. This is your holy void.

—

What is so significant about being in nonverbal consciousness? I have been practicing and putting my attention on my attention. I do experience a peaceful and undefined awareness that I think you would call nonverbal consciousness. I do not get any significant benefits from this perception. It is so ordinary and with no obvious importance in my life.
The way you formulate your statement indicates that you are putting attention on your thoughts in order to get some significant benefits in your life. You are not in your attention, which is void of any judgments. The mind thinks that it is so ordinary, without benefit and without importance. Our mind is governed by personal ambition. It wants to have not ordinary but extraordinary experiences or sensations. Indeed, paying attention to our attention is ordinary. It is not an exercise to be practiced to gain some benefits. It is done out of a need to learn about our consciousness. If it is done with this need in mind, it is enough to do it once or initially a few times to learn that our attention is nonverbal and always present. From what you said, it appears that your attention is, for the most part, in your thinking mind, not in your nonverbal attention.

—

I want to know consciousness. What words can I use to define consciousness intellectually?
Words cannot be used to define it.

Why?

Consciousness makes intellectual definitions possible. The intellect defines objects. Consciousness is not an object.

I do not follow this. I simply want to know what I can say about consciousness.

Intellectually, you can say what consciousness is not.

Why?

Consciousness is noticed directly without intellectual definitions. Intellectual definitions of consciousness are words. To know consciousness, you do not need words. But if you say consciousness is not something that the intellect can define, then your attention automatically shifts to notice that you are consciousness.

———

What is nonverbal consciousness?

It is the unchanging, constant consciousness we have at birth and throughout our life. It is labeled nonverbal to distinguish it from our conceptual or verbal thinking that is commonly called consciousness.

Why is it important to know about it?

Once we realize that our consciousness is nonverbal, we cease to expect spiritual knowledge from thinking and recognize thinking as an acquired survival skill.

What is the advantage of realizing this?

Our attention is no longer trapped in mythological beliefs inherited from cultural traditions. Instead, it is free to be aware of our divine innate consciousness, or God-given consciousness.

———

Our attention is nonverbal. When we pay attention to our attention, we are in our nonverbal consciousness. Is this so?

Yes, it is so.

I attempted to do this, and I agree that I am in my consciousness, which appears to be nonverbal. So far, so good. But when you define this nonverbal consciousness as divine consciousness or even God-given consciousness, I have a problem. How can we say that it is divine or God-given consciousness? It is a hollow assumption.

Listen. We did not create this consciousness, and we know nobody else created it or gave it to us. According to cultural convention, we label it divine or God-given consciousness. It does not matter what it is labeled. What matters is to realize that our consciousness is nonverbal and present in the form of our attention.

———

What is the definition of life? Or how is life understood?

There is nothing but consciousness. There is no other existence. Therefore, we can also say that there is life, nothing else.

This is very general and convenient. Is there anything more specific?

When the world is viewed with the conceptual mind, things appear separate from each other. This is a fragmented view of the world. That is why you ask for specifics. Inquiry demonstrates that to perceive the world nonverbally gives us a view in which the unity and mutual interdependence of every form of existence becomes evident. This is labeled as the undifferentiated perception of reality. To answer your question, I can give you the specifics involved in the perception of this unity, so listen. The principles that govern the biological life of people, animals, plants, insects, and single cell organisms are no different from the principles that govern subatomic particles, quantum particles, and our heavenly bodies. Therefore, stars, planets, galaxies, and the elements in space, such as photons, neutrinos, gravitons, dark matter, and other not-yet-labeled elements, are part of life, like you and me, like animals and plants. They, and us, form the living body of this infinite universe, which is nothing else but living divine consciousness. This consciousness is existence, and there is no other. And that is, succinctly, the essence of how life is perceived.

———

I read we can have inner bliss only when we are free from thoughts and that this is our true nature.
This statement clearly says we experience bliss when we realize that our true nature is nonverbal consciousness, not our thoughts.
How do I become free from thoughts?
Freedom from thoughts is a realization that occurs through inquiry into consciousness, referred to as the I-inquiry or *who am I* question. When you familiarize yourself with this *I*, you learn that it has little in common with your thoughts. It is the permanent consciousness you have from the time you are born. This consciousness is nonverbal. Thought-consciousness is a collection of acquired verbal meanings about yourself. When you realize that you are nonverbal consciousness, you abandon those thoughts about yourself. This condition is referred to as freedom from thoughts. Your nonverbal awareness is inner bliss.

———

How do we know what is the ego and what is the Self, with a capital *S*—Atman in Sanskrit—or what you call nonverbal self? Let me say it differently. Is there a specific concrete feeling within us to tell us the difference between the ego and the nonverbal self?

Yes. You feel a concrete mental sensation when your physical or psychological well-being is under threat. Don't you?

Yes.

That is your ego.

I understand that. But how do I know or concretely feel my nonverbal self?

You concretely feel your nonverbal self when you put your attention on your attention. The ego manifests itself as a mental sensation, and the nonverbal self is a mute awareness of your nonverbal attention.

———

If our attention is nonverbal and the realization of it is without mental sensations, how do we know it exists?

When you know something exists, mental sensations are not always present. For example, when you say *I am*, do you have mental sensations? No, you do not. In the same way, when we acknowledge that our own attention is nonverbal, we do not experience any mental sensations. Do we?

Oh, I see. It is extremely subtle.

Most of us overlook this and consider it unimportant, without any obvious significance. We ignore it because it is so subtle. But this subtle awareness of our nonverbal attention is our consciousness.

But if one does not realize how subtle it is, like I did not, one will never understand nonverbal consciousness. Is this why it remains so obscure?

It is probably one of the reasons. Our consciousness is nonverbal, but most of us have been conditioned to believe that thinking is our consciousness. Since awareness of our attention is without mental sensations, it takes a certain mental stability to accept the significance of this type of subtlety. When people hear that you need to put your attention on your attention, they expect it to be either a mental exercise or meditation technique. Our culturally programmed impulse is to first engage our thinking ability. We believe that we will achieve some favorable results by using our mind.

What is the best way to put our attention on the attention?

It is the same as asking *who am I*. It is part of the I-inquiry, an act of introspection. We are trying to understand our attention. Our attention is the same as the nonverbal self, which understandably carries an obscure meaning for many people. To be aware of our attention is easy. If we put our attention on it, we realize that it is nonverbal. Once we notice this, we realize that our verbal knowledge about ourselves, such as I am so-and-so or that my role in life is this or that, is absurd or irrelevant, and it fades away. We realize that thoughts restrict us by defining us verbally. We are unknown to our own thoughts. We recognize that we are pure nonverbal consciousness.

Why is it important to know this?

Knowing this is not enough. This needs to be realized. Then our actions no longer depend only on mental decisions but also are linked to our nonverbal awareness. This fundamental transformation results from the seemingly insignificant realization that our unassuming and silent attention is our consciousness.

I understand that God is only an idea in my mind, but so is everything else I think of in the entire world. The world is also an idea in my mind. Is there anything we know that is not an idea or a concept in our mind?
No, there is no such thing because to know is an act of the mind. Everything in our mind is an idea.
Then if God, the world, and everything else are only ideas in our mind, how do we know that they really exist? I understand how God is just an idea in our mind since nobody sees God in physical form. But the world is physical, and everybody sees it. It is hard to believe that the world is merely an idea in our mind.
Listen carefully. This requires your full attention. Your statement that the world is physical and everybody sees it is also an idea in your mind. Other people may have similar perceptions, but we know about other people also as an idea in our mind. Everything we see is our own idea. There is a school of philosophy called solipsism that claims the existence we can be sure of is our own existence and everything else is an idea in our mind. Whereas with awareness of nonverbal consciousness, there is nothing but existence. Nonexistence cannot be conceived. This existence is an undifferentiated universal consciousness that includes you and me. We see the world as an idea, but knowing about the world as an idea does not mean it does not exist. It means that we know segments of this existence as ideas. This understanding is possible when we realize that we are undifferentiated consciousness. With this realization, our attention stays in undifferentiated nonverbal awareness. This knowing is not dependent on the thinking mind.

I came across the unusual statement that to think is not your real nature. How much more opposed to common sense can a statement be? And yet I have a gut feeling that this statement is right.

Go with your gut feeling. So what does this statement mean to us? That is the question, yes?

Yes.

To think is not your real nature is essentially the same as saying that thinking is not your consciousness.

If thinking is not our real nature, then what is our real nature? My reading involves thinking, and it is very much my nature. I enjoy it.

Understanding this statement is possible after uncovering our nonverbal consciousness, which we have at birth prior to the mental conditioning we receive from our cultural training. The ability to read is the main part of this training. So how do we uncover our nonverbal consciousness?

That is precisely what my reading is supposed to do. I am expecting that one day I will read something so wonderful that I will be flooded with enlightenment.

One day you may turn your attention to yourself.

I am already doing this and that is why I want to talk about it.

Talking about it is not the same as turning your attention to yourself.

I am afraid to look into myself. There is nothing there. I like to say that it is boring, but actually I am afraid.

Realize what you said. Your fear is the label you put on the feeling of nothing there. This nothing is the firm nonverbal divine consciousness with which you are born. Think about it logically. Who sees this nothing? It is you yourself who is there and nobody else. This nothing is you, yourself, as nonverbal consciousness where there is no thinking.

———

When I ask myself *who am I*, my answer is always I am my mind. I would like to believe that I am something more exotic, but no, the answer is always the same. This is disappointing.
What happens when you are aware that you exist, which is the knowledge of *I am*?
I am mentally aware that I am. My mind tells me that I am or that I exist.
What happens when you do not pay attention to your mind? Do you still know that you exist?
Yes.
How do you know that?
I do not know, but I know that I am. I exist.
So you see, not everything about you is known with your mind.
Oh, I see.
So when you ask yourself again *who am I*, you may add "I do not know" to what your mind knows. There is a lot that your mind knows and also some that your mind does not know. When you say that you are your mind, you imply that you are in your mind. The opposite is true. You are not your mind, and you are not in your mind: the mind is in you.
René Descartes said, *"Cogito, ergo sum,"* or "I think, therefore I am." Doesn't this phrase imply that I am my mind?
This cultural platitude is an intellectual misconception prevalent among most philosophers. A stricter logical statement would be the reverse. *Sum, ergo cogito.* I am, therefore I think. First you must exist. Then you can think.

So Descartes was wrong?

In the confines and limitations of conceptual thought, his statement "I think, therefore I am" is logical. But this statement by itself, out of conceptual context, is wrong.

What would be the right way to say this?

We can say I am aware of my existence without thinking, but I need thinking to label it in order to talk about it.

Oh, I see. Isn't it rather awkward?

It is awkward but accurate. There is a fundamental difference between the nonverbal approach and philosophy. In philosophy the notion of *I am* is a concept in the mind, and concepts are believed to be realities. Such beliefs are the source of disappointment because they are ideas in the mind, not nonverbal realizations. With awareness of nonverbal consciousness, the *I am* is an awareness present within us prior to thinking and while we are thinking. The *I am* is not a concept but a label, a symbol for communication purposes.

Then how can I know about who I am prior to thinking?

You already know it. You said you do not know how, but you know that you exist. Shift your attention to your existence instead of your thoughts. To pay attention to your existence is to know who you are. You are existence.

What is so special about knowing that I am existence or that I exist?

To know you are existence or you exist without relying on thinking means you know that you are not your mind. The mind is an acquired instrument. It is not you.

———

I would like to discuss the notion of experience. I have been

reading spiritual literature for over a decade, and each time I come to what I think would be my understanding, I am told that true understanding is really experienced. I am told that notions like realization, liberation, and enlightenment are understood only when experienced. Intellectual clarity is important to me. I was raised in a strict religious environment, and early on I understood that my faith is almost exclusively based on mythology. I must admit that some of those myths can be very attractive, but some of them can be like a horror movie. At best they are entertaining for children but fall short when it comes to appealing to mature individuals of the twenty-first century. What is the difference between understanding and experience?

Your question is in line with the inquiry process.

I am familiar with the investigative aspect of nonverbal awareness, and this is what attracts me to it. I am a scientist, fully aware of the value of inquiry in scientific matters. In the newest advances of theoretical physics, the line between the objective physical world and subjective world of consciousness is not only being questioned but is rapidly disappearing or, I would even say, has altogether disappeared. We do not know what this new reality is, and we do not have an appropriate label for it.

Similar concerns have already been considered and discussed in the Upanishads thousands of years before Christ. The label for this new reality has been coined as non-differentiated reality.

Yes, yes. I read about this. It is a beautiful label. I understand so much when I read, but still I . . .

I know what you were about to say: But still, I do not have an experience of it.

Exactly.

Your scientific training helps you to clearly grasp the intellectual point of the inquiry process. You can imagine subtle concepts like space-time or one quantum particle being in two places simultaneously, called entanglement, and the concept of non-differentiated reality.

Yes, I know. Some scientists refer to entanglement as *spooky behavior*. I can easily imagine the non-differentiated reality in my mind, but whoever thought of it in the Upanishads must have experienced it before the formulation of this label. Mental imagination alone leaves me empty-handed.

Being empty-handed is a known, well-defined point in the usual sequence of the inquiry.

I often do the inquiry without fulfilling results. I need to know how I can jump from mere mental understanding to knowing from experience.

Maybe the reason you cannot make the jump is that you expect your experience to be a verbal, conceptual event. Experience is the result of what is called the *nonverbal experience* or *nonverbal realization*.

Yes, I read about this nonverbal experience, but frankly, I do not know what that is. Sometimes I even suspect that it is a smoke screen for some writers to hide their inability to cope with the issue. It may just be an easy way out to say, oh well, that is nonverbal.

Yes, it will appear that way until you have the nonverbal experience yourself. Inquiry can give you a nonverbal experience. The common conceptual experience of the mind is a recognizable verbal sensation. The nonverbal experience is a quiet realization of a presence, without recognizable sensations.

Can I really do that?

Maybe it is simpler than you think. It is not so much as doing it but knowing where to look and how to look. Being aware of where your attention is looking is the key.

What do you mean by that?

As I indicated earlier, we expect to have a conceptual answer instead of something new and, at first, something unknown. We are used to having recognizable, familiar sensations in the form of slightly modified ideas that accompany intellectual investigations. Such investigations stay within the scope of a known conceptual mental realm that is limited by definitions of words or symbols. In this inquiry, do not expect any verbal sensations. There are none. The reason there are none is that you are going to inquire into the nonverbal aspect of yourself, which you have from birth. Our mind does not notice it because the mind notices concepts, whereas now we are interested in applying our inquiry to focus on nonconceptual consciousness. If the mind cannot follow us and cannot help us, then who or what can help us? The inquiry process, of course, and that is exactly why we have it.

Are you not using your mind now, which is verbal, to talk about the nonverbal inquiry?

Yes, the inquiry is initiated by the mind. Once the inquiry starts, the mind is useless. Even the inquiry itself becomes redundant when the outcome is successful. What is a successful outcome? We are really going after knowing or discovering the makeup of the inquirer—more specifically, who or what is the self or the *I*. Knowing this will put conceptual knowledge in proper perspective. This is the ultimate success described in the Upanishads, which I am sure you read.

Oh yes, many times. It says after knowing the self, everything else becomes known.

That is right.

I often felt that this statement in the Upanishads is an exaggeration. You, however, just said that knowing the self would put conceptual knowledge in proper perspective. Can you explain?

This statement refers to spiritual knowledge. If taken out of context, it may be considered an exaggeration. The scientific knowledge and the day-to-day utilitarian knowledge will stay the same, but our attitude changes. We no longer consider mental knowledge as absolute. It is understood as useful and relative. But of course, this happens after the discovery of our *I*. The purpose of this inquiry is to identify the permanent existence of nonverbal consciousness. We are born with it, and it is with us our entire life. The conceptual mind cannot see it because it is nonverbal. How can we know about it? We can know about it as a presence without the usual verbal sensations that accompany mental cognition. How is it done? It is accomplished by using inquiry questions that bypass our conceptual mind. Why do we need to bypass the mind? It is because verbal sensations of the mind distract our nonverbal perceptions. What are those inquiry questions? I will give you several of them. First, do you have to think to know that you exist, or do you know it without thinking?

I do not know. I have to think about it.

Are you noticing what happened? You automatically, out of habit, went to use your conceptual mind.

Yes, I did.

So you have learned something new. Make a note of it. I will rephrase the same question. That awareness you have of *I am*, is it the result of thinking or do you experience it without thinking?

I . . . I really do not know.

Not to know is good. Take note of it because not knowing is useful knowledge too. So now, the next inquiry question, when you wake up from sleep, how do you know that you were asleep?

I remember myself before I fell asleep.

Well, that is remembering yourself when you were awake. The question is, listen carefully, how do you know that you were asleep.

During sleep? I do not remember anything during sleep.

Who is the one who does not remember?

I am the one.

So you admit that you were present during sleep.

Yes, I do. I do not remember who I was or how I was there, but I was there.

All right. Take note of that too. Then here is the next inquiry question. Can you imagine a time—any time, past, present, or future—in which you do not exist, or you are not there?

Yes, I can. I am not in the future.

Whose future is it?

It is my future. Oh I see. I am there in my own future too.

So you realize that you cannot think yourself out of existence.

Yes, I realize that . . . only now.

Thus far, you can notice a common thread. You are present in many circumstances, and yet your conceptual mind does not even know about it. Also, your mind does not know who or what is this *I* and when or how it is present. So one more question, *who am I*?

I really do not know. I repeat, I do not know. I have been asking this question so many times and for so long.

Let me ask you, who does not know who you are?

I do.

You see, no matter what you say, such as I know or I don't know or you acknowledge or deny something or imagine or question or even sleep or do anything with your consciousness, the *I* is always there. And yet your mind does not know that the *I* is permanently there, and your mind does not even know what your *I* is. And most importantly, your mind is not capable of eliminating your *I* from existence. So the mind is ineffective when confronted by the *I*. The mind is oblivious to it because your *I* is nonverbal. Being nonverbal, do not expect a mental sensation as if it were a concept. It is not a concept. Your *I* is a solid presence, formless and silent. Your *I* was there before the formation of your conceptual mind. This nonverbal presence of the conscious *I* is the experience of your nonverbal self. Here is the difference between understanding and experience. Understanding is about grasping the meaning of spiritual concepts. Experience is the awareness of our nonverbal undifferentiated consciousness.

———

Why do we need beliefs?
Culturally indoctrinated minds feel uncomfortable without beliefs. And yet ironically, when the mind is emptied of all beliefs, we experience nonverbal wholeness. Our innate nonverbal consciousness exists without beliefs. When we know this, we are free from mental beliefs. We are born without beliefs, and we can live without beliefs. We do not need beliefs.

———

Can you give a simplified course on the I-inquiry?
All right. The I-inquiry requires an alert intellect. Listen carefully. The notion of *I* is selected for the inquiry because the *I* is the first idea that comes into our mind. This means that without

the idea of *I* you cannot have any other thoughts. Also, you need to know that you are aware of your existence nonverbally, without the need to think. So the importance of *I* and the ability to notice the presence of nonverbal awareness are the two requirements needed to have a successful I-inquiry. If you do not know this, spend some time observing your consciousness before you start the inquiry.

I know this and I understand this.

Good. For example, when we have disturbing thoughts, the first question would be, who is the thinker who has these thoughts?

I would say me.

So from now on your attention must stay, as long as needed, on the one who is me. If you are focused, you would soon notice that you have no idea who or what your me is, no idea what you are looking at, and no idea what this whole process is for. You may even be frustrated. Continue looking, and if you feel lost, it is fine. You feel lost because you expect to have a mental answer to your question. Instead, all you know is that you have no idea. Well, that is exactly right. You have no idea, and really you cannot have any idea. You see nothing. At this point you can ask who or what is this me or *I* who is looking at nothing, and the inquiry will go back to the starting point. Or, better, use your observation skill and notice the reason you see nothing is that you are involved in a nonverbal perception of nonverbal consciousness. Why is it so? Because if it were not your own consciousness, you would not know that you see nothing. Seeing nothing is being in your own nonverbal consciousness. It is your consciousness that sees nothing. You did not suddenly disappear. You are still here.

This is where I get stuck and confused. I do not see the importance of this. It is so ordinary.

Do you expect something extraordinary?

Yes. I read that the discovery of the Self, with a capital *S*, which you call nonverbal self, is the most wonderful experience. I am expecting that at the conclusion of this inquiry I will have that experience.

What you say indicates that you are interested in self-aggrandizement. The I-inquiry is about self-knowledge. Verbal or conceptual descriptions of nonverbal states of consciousness keep you restricted to an intellectual understanding that needs to be abandoned.

How can I do that?

You said you are aware of your existence without the help of words or thoughts. Is that so?

Yes, it is. I do know that.

Listen. When you face the existence of your own consciousness looking at your own nothingness and you are the one who is experiencing this, you decide that it is too ordinary for you. You are right. It is ordinary. Listen carefully. Do not expect any magic or miracle. There is nothing more ordinary than the perception of your own nonverbal consciousness. And because your consciousness is nonverbal, it cannot be perceived like a thought or word. It can be acknowledged as the presence of your attention. No matter where you end up in your inquiry, your attention will always be there because that attention is your own existence, which you cannot deny. That existence of your attention is the nonverbal self. Notice carefully what I am saying. That existence of your attention is the nonverbal self. That existence of your attention is not different from your nonverbal consciousness or from the nonverbal self. In the nonverbal realm there are no conceptual differentiations that you are used to when you perceive the world through divisive ideas.

Existence, attention, consciousness, and nonverbal self are not separate ideas. There are no ideas here. We need to use words to talk about it. However, you cannot know this nonverbal reality using words. So again, one more time: This existence is the nonverbal self, and you cannot deny your own existence. Do not expect something fantastic that you read about in books. Expectation blocks the perception of this most ordinary nonverbal consciousness always present as your attention. This realization occurs in silence without any trace in your thoughts, leaving you speechless, unable to describe it. Once you discover this, you will have no need for any further inquiry.

——

What is instinct? Is nonverbal consciousness the same or similar to instinct in humans and maybe even in animals?
Humans, animals, plants, insects, and microscopic life, as well as inanimate matter, share the same consciousness. There is nothing but consciousness. The diversity we experience with our senses are phenomenal forms of that consciousness. Instinct is a form of that consciousness.

I am an anthropologist. In most so-called primitive religions and animistic traditions, life is celebrated as divine. In Judaism, Christianity, and Islam, animal life has been discredited in favor of a monotheistic belief in one abstract God invented by our intellect. If all life shares the same consciousness, why do the major Western religions not accept this?
As an anthropologist you must know that monotheism is a sociopolitical device used by religious leaders to unite people under a common belief system. Also, belief in one God makes people

dependent on those who claim to know about this particular God. The primary concern of those leaders is social unity, social stability, and the physical welfare of communities, not spiritual accuracy.

I know that. Monotheism was already known in ancient civilizations like Mesopotamia and Egypt before it became part of the Bible. During the fourth century, Rome conveniently adopted only monotheistic branches of Christianity and made monotheism the official faith of its highly controlled and regimented empire. Roman religious authorities systematically eliminated other forms of Christianity—for example, Gnosticism—to safeguard control over preferred beliefs. How do you view the belief in God?

Belief in one God is a fragmented and narrow intellectual understanding of divinity. It excludes one part of existence and favors another. We do not realize that every form of life is necessary to support our own life, and every form of life is divine. Conceptual information can be successfully used in our utilitarian endeavors, but the value of concepts is limited to mental understanding. Intellectual beliefs in general, including the belief in one God or many gods, have no significant impact on spiritual realization.

Organized religions are based on mental abstract principles, aren't they?

Yes. They are based on conceptual structures formulated by the mind. Our mental understanding of the world, which we get from our civilization, has become so developed through the ages that it has overshadowed our innate nonverbal consciousness.

How do you see the divine or God?

The belief that God or divinity is separate from the world or us is an intellectual concept. The realization of divinity is not the result of mental or rational definitions. It is a state of nonverbal awareness. This condition gives us the apperception of undifferentiated reality, which is structurally divine. Divinity is not separate from the world and us. Neither is divinity in the world or in us. Divinity is existence.

Your description of divinity is very similar to the description of the Great Spirit of Native North American shamans. It is also like the notion of God from the Dream World of Aboriginal Australian shamans. I would venture to say that most probably it is the same among all shamans of the world. You say it takes nonverbal awareness to perceive divinity. I call this instinctive perception of reality. Back to my original question, is awareness of our nonverbal consciousness the same as instinct?

Yes, the way you define the meaning of instinct, yes, it is the same.

———

What prevents us from being aware of our nonverbal consciousness?

It is prevented by our expectation that it can be known by the thoughts of our mind. This expectation is futile because thoughts, being external and alien to our consciousness, are not capable of this. So inadvertently, this expectation blocks the awareness of our nonverbal consciousness.

Why do we do that?

Out of unconscious habit, attention is given exclusively to thoughts instead of including attention to attention, which is your nonverbal consciousness. Your attention can focus on thoughts and on the attention itself. Our attention can do this intermittently and simultaneously. Use this ability.

Do you think that the mind needs to be destroyed to be aware of our nonverbal consciousness?

Why do we need to destroy the mind?

That is what I read.

You need your mind to function in the world. Leave the mind as it is. What is meant by *destroyed* is the recognition that the mind is not your consciousness. This acknowledgment is the so-called destruction of the mind.

So the mind can remain as it is. Only my attitude changes.

Yes.

But how is it that we do not know about nonverbal consciousness in our daily life?

It is due to the conditioned habit of where you put your attention in your daily life.

Can we break this habit?

Yes, you can do it through the process of inquiry.

How is I-inquiry practiced?

I-inquiry is not practiced like a spiritual discipline. When you understand what it is, you will spontaneously do the inquiry as the need arises.

Many, many times in my long life I have wondered, what is life or death, life after death, or eternity? Is there a present moment, or what is the meaning of passage of time? Is there

time at all, is there space, or what is space-time? Is there a parallel universe? Is the singularity of black holes a wormhole to other dimensions? If the world is made from quantum particles, what is beyond them? I could go on and on. The amount of topics to wonder about is endless. Could you talk about some of these subjects?

Where would you like me to start?

I am mostly interested in eternity. This may cover it all.

So you want to talk about eternity. Are you aware that ideas, including eternity, are concepts in your imagination?

I suppose it is imagination, although I think of them as mental concepts that represent reality.

Is the concept of eternity a conceptual reality for you?

Yes, it is.

But would you agree with me if I say that the word *eternity* is a conceptual reality and does not carry anything else within itself?

No, I wouldn't. I expect that this concept represents a reality in our world.

You attribute a reality to it without realizing that what you have is a concept and you have nothing to show for it.

Yes, that is exactly right. It is very frustrating.

Concepts describe reality. They are not reality. It is a significant difference to bear in mind. But because our linguistic arsenal is filled with concepts, we can assume that they describe some sort of reality.

Does this mean that I need to experience eternity? How is that possible?

It is possible, and it is necessary. Otherwise, you are going to be stuck with the concept of eternity, well, for eternity. There must be some reason for this interest since the notion of eternity has been used frequently in recorded history. So I will tell you how it is possible to experience eternity. When you investigate your consciousness, you know that you exist. But can you yourself conceive of a time when you did not exist? You cannot deny your own existence. Nobody can. It is not possible to deny your own *I*. Logically, you cannot deny the denier.

How does this relate to eternity?

We are halfway there. If you know that you are firmly established in your own consciousness, and you cannot get rid of your existence even if you try, the next question is, what do you know about your *I*.

I know practically nothing.

Well, to fully understand the meaning of eternity, you have to first know the means necessary to know it. Therefore, you must be acquainted with your *I* who wants to know about eternity. To begin this process, ask yourself who is that *I* who is trying to know about eternity. At first, you may see nothing. If you do not, try again until you see nothing. It is important to see nothing because our mind avoids seeing nothing. The mind usually pays attention to words or meaningful concepts. When you see nothing, ask yourself who sees nothing. Your answer will probably be I do. At this point you realize that although you see nothing, your *I* is still present. When your awareness is established in this always present *I*, you realize that this *I* is the nonverbal consciousness you are at birth. This consciousness is the experience of eternity. When you realize your innate consciousness is nonverbal, you are in eternity in the present moment. Your nonverbal consciousness is eternal. Why? Because our consciousness is the same as the eternal universal consciousness. This awareness of your nonverbal consciousness in the present moment is the realization that eternity is all there is. This is not an idea or a concept. It is the experience that we are part of a universe that is eternal.

——

I wonder what place God has when we are aware of our nonverbal consciousness. I believe in all religions of the world. They speak of the same God, although they use different words to describe Him. So far I have read about the major religions, and now I am going to read about Shamans (of Shamanism), Druids, Sun Worshippers, Moon Worshippers, Gnostics, who say that they experience God within, and agnostics, who say that they do not know about God. I read about atheists, who say that there is no God. I noticed that some books on spirituality speak of God freely, but some seem to question the value of believing. What is your position regarding belief in God?

Let me comment on atheism. We seek to explain the mystery of creation. Our mind will always find a way to satisfy that need in one way or another. Atheists replace the word *God* with terms like *nature, energy, force, matter, universe,* and the like. To say there is no God and to say there is God are both beliefs.

I am glad that you are saying this about atheists. Lately, I have been thinking the same way. But then why not just use the word *God*?

They object to the word *God* the same way you object to the word *nature* or *universe*. Our disagreements are confined within verbal meanings. We do not realize that the mystery of this life cannot be explained by relying on meanings available in our language.

So then what can we rely on?

If this question is pursued, it will inevitably lead to the discovery of the limitations of our verbal understanding. We instinctively feel that words are not adequate to give us full comprehension of the meaning of life. This is the main reason we have such a huge diversity of creeds. On the level of verbal understanding, the field is wide open for any creed, even nefarious beliefs. Most major religions are based on verbal beliefs. Some monastic orders as well as some shamanic and pagan religions try to go beyond the confines of mental understanding. Gnostics clearly speak of nonverbal experience of the divine through gnosis or insight. It is on this personal insight that we need to rely, not on words.

I see.

Nonverbal consciousness is not a religion. It does not require any belief in a divinity. As you know, most religions state that the divine is separate from the world and humankind. With awareness of nonverbal consciousness there is no division between humankind, the world, and divinity. To help realize this, we follow a process of inquiry into the origin of our conviction that there is a separate me within us. It is the me that says I am separate from the world and God. Therefore, the need to know what is that me arises. Once the me is understood to be a concept, the division between man, world, and God stops for good.

In many scriptures God is spoken of as separate and above us humans.

As you know, those scriptures describe God as omnipresent. If this is so, then they are essentially saying that there is no separation between the world, God, and us.

I never thought of it that way.

Intellectual clarity is needed if we want to understand our

phenomenal existence. Therefore, there is the need to examine, investigate, and inquire into our own consciousness. If we do not know ourselves first, what we know may be distorted by our desires, insecurities, or cultural biases.

Since nonverbal consciousness is not a religion, can anybody practice it?

Yes, but there are no rituals to practice. You can follow your own religious practices and at the same time use the method of inquiry.

This is different and new to me. What exactly is that method?

This method is the inquiry into the me. In short, it is labeled *I-inquiry*. This system was developed at the dawn of civilization and came to us through the ancient Sanskrit writings known as the Upanishads. Ever since, it has been a living tradition among spiritually minded people. Although it originated in India, today it is known in many countries.

Is there something like that in the West?

Yes. Gnostics use I-inquiry. You read about them.

But they are a religion. They speak of Christ.

Their inquiry method is the same. The inquiry is what matters, not the labels. When the inquiry into the self is successful, the results are the same. People of all faiths can find divinity within or, better yet, discover and realize that there is no division between the world, God, and us. God is truly omnipresent. Still better, God is all there is.

What is I-inquiry about?

It is called inquiry into the *I* because the *I* is present in our every thought. Therefore, investigating our thoughts or our faith or any of our beliefs is the same as investigating the self or *I*.

Does investigating my faith mean questioning it? If so, I do not want to do this. I am comfortable with it, and I am proud

that my religious belief is universal and accepting of all faiths. If more people were like me, we would have a peaceful world. I fear that you question the value of belief in God. Is this true? Could you explain your position regarding the existence of God? This is my number one question.

God is all there is. It is more meaningful if this is not a conceptual belief but a realization in your nonverbal being to the point that you do not feel any separation from Him and from the world. We pay attention to the verbal meaning of our beliefs instead of the believer. To know the believer counts more than the beliefs. People have differing beliefs but similar aspirations. We want to know God. Mental concepts about God are what divide us. For many of us, those concepts are acquired in childhood from our cultural conditioning that has never been examined and that we blindly defend. If we rely on these concepts our knowledge about God is limited to the confines of ideas in our mind. God, the world, and us are not separate. This is possible to realize when we no longer rely on conceptual beliefs.

———

I cannot control my restless thoughts. I read that it is possible to stop thinking. Can I stop thinking?

You cannot stop thinking by deciding to stop thinking because this decision is another thought, which adds more thinking.

Why do you speak of void and silence?

Void and silence are not the result of your decision to stop thinking. You need to find who cannot control these thoughts, whose thoughts they are, or who wants to stop thinking. You cannot rely on reading alone. You need to get involved experientially. Otherwise, you will endlessly continue shuffling ideas you read about. The first step is to find who is this *I* who wants this. Once you do that, the rest will follow by itself. Thinking can spontaneously stop when you know who you are.

———

I have read that when an inquiry is performed correctly, the mind disappears. How is it possible?
This statement refers to the realization that the mind does not exist independently from our nonverbal self. Through inquiry we learn that the mind is not an independent entity but is a form of dynamic verbal consciousness, dependent on our nonverbal consciousness. The mind as an independent entity is said to disappear through inquiry, but the mind as conscious mental energy cannot disappear because it is part of our nonverbal makeup. When the mind is understood to be part of our nonverbal consciousness, our perception changes. There is no disappearance of any sort.

———

I read that killing the mind and the ego is necessary for spiritual realization. Can you explain why?
First, understand that the mind and the ego are the same. No, it is not an oversimplification. The ego or *I* is the common denominator in our thoughts, the pivotal first notion that the mind depends on and revolves around. When you kill the ego, you kill the mind. The idea of killing, however, is an exaggeration, an archaic remnant from the Upanishads, which were written in a direct, honest, but blunt style. It means the neutralization of our mind's influence on spiritual awareness. This is not done by

the mind or ego directly. It is done through a process of inquiry that reveals the mind and ego are not self-generated entities but a form of dynamic energy of our consciousness. This consciousness is nonverbal and is labeled the nonverbal self. It is always present within us and is the foundation for the operation of our mind and ego. Through this discovery, we shift our attention from mental activities to nonverbal consciousness. This condition can be labeled as killing of mind and ego. However, it is really the shifting of our attention. The ego and mind are still there but latent, waiting to be used for practical needs. Mind and ego are useful instruments. When we understand the role of the mind and ego, we respect them. But no amount of explaining can replace the actual realization of the nonverbal self. You yourself can answer your question when you actually perform your own inquiry by asking where the ego and mind originate. Or ask where your *I* is coming from.

I read how to do this inquiry, tried it many times, and nothing happens.

You say that nothing happens, yes?

Yes.

There is someone who is aware of that nothing. Who is it? You see, the one who is aware of this nothing is your own consciousness. It feels like nothing because it is a nonverbal type of consciousness. When you give it careful attention, you realize that this nothing is your nonverbal consciousness.

——

I have a very strong attraction to the idea of emptiness. I do not know what it is, but I always have a sense of well-being when I think of it. Once and for all, I would like to understand the

meaning of emptiness that is often mentioned in spiritual writings in the East as well as in the West.

What do you understand by the word *emptiness*?

I must say that I really do not know what this word means. I only know that I like it. Why do mystics, gurus, spiritual masters, and even poets mention it? What do they mean by it?

It refers to mental emptiness, not absolute emptiness.

What is mental emptiness?

It is a condition of the mind when it is empty of thoughts.

There must be something there when thoughts are not there.

Yes, exactly. When thoughts are not there, the mind is full of non-verbal consciousness. It is this nonverbal consciousness that is labeled by mystics as emptiness.

What is nonverbal consciousness?

It is the divine consciousness with which you are born.

How can I know it?

Your wanting to know is an unquestioned belief that we can know everything with our thinking mind. But since this consciousness is nonverbal, you cannot know it with your mind. It is not a thought.

How do you know it?

I do not know it mentally, but I notice it as a presence in my attention. It is this presence that is our nonverbal consciousness.

Can I notice it too?

Yes, you can. Instead of putting your attention on your mental idea of emptiness as you usually do, put your attention on your attention.

You mean to put my attention on my attention?

Yes.

____

Do we need a guru to understand spirituality? Some spiritual literature seems to overemphasize the importance of a guru.
In Hindu religious traditions—for example, Vedanta—the emphasis on the need for a guru is a strong mythological belief. If you think that spirituality can be taught mentally, then a guru may be needed. Here we are trying to understand spirituality within one's own consciousness. The awareness that we are born with divine nonverbal consciousness is spiritual realization. A guru is not needed for this realization.

My other question is about individuality as expressed by our notion of myself or me. In Western thought this notion is never questioned, but in spiritual literature it is often stated that the me does not exist. How could that be? This statement bothers me. I experience myself every day.
Listen carefully. The notion of me is part of language. Our language is part of thinking. Thinking is a mental survival tool acquired from our civilization. The me is necessary for thinking itself. Without this me, thinking would not be possible. Denying or accepting the existence of me has no relevance to our innate spiritual consciousness. We are born without language.

I read that the body is a mental projection. What does that mean?
This is just a graphic way of saying that the mind sees the world in segments called ideas. In your example the mind separates our body from the rest of the world and makes a concept called body.

———

After many years of studying major world religions and a variety of minor faiths, I came to realize that almost all of them

are based on mythological beliefs in the supernatural. It is a big surprise and personal disappointment. I wonder why, after thousands of years, humanity did not succeed to shake off religious mythological beliefs, whereas in sociopolitical and scientific fields there seem to be many revolutionary achievements. I am thrilled you do not advocate any mythological beliefs and instead focus on the use of our rational mind in conjunction with spiritual inquiry.

As you stated, most religions are based on mythological beliefs in the supernatural. The influence of mythology extends into ordinary daily beliefs that we never question. For example, where did you get the notion that the belief in God is a normal condition in the makeup of your thoughts? Do you know?

I never questioned this. Is it from our mythology?

Yes, it is taken from mythology, part of an ancient belief in the supernatural. So you were prompted to study religions by your mythological convictions, and you ended up discovering that religions are nothing more than mythologies. Your mind may be trapped in mythology, and you are asking why humanity is trapped in it too. Do you see the dilemma your mind can be in?

Are you sure that the belief in God comes from mythology?

Listen carefully. To believe in God you need to believe that God is separate from you. Belief in separation is an arbitrary assumption made ages ago by our ancestors. You are born without beliefs. This means that the belief in God is superimposed on our innate consciousness. In other words, believing in God is believing in the supernatural, which, as you know, is called mythology. There is a difference between believing in a divinity that is offered by traditional religions and the urge to know the divine empirically within ourselves where belief is not involved. Do you follow?

Yes, I do.

Our first concern needs to be to know who we are. To know who I am leads to the realization of divinity without mythological beliefs. So when you refer to yourself as *I*, do you know what this *I* is?

No, I do not know.

Listen. Pay attention to who says I do not know. You want to know who is there who says this. If you ask who knows that you do not know, you have no choice but to acknowledge that this *who* is yourself. This is your *I*. This acknowledgment is the realization of your innate nonverbal consciousness, which is referred to as the nonverbal self. It cannot be identified conceptually. It has no form or dimension. If it did, it would be part of our mental knowledge. Although the mind is absent in perceiving it, the mind remains unchanged and intact. What changes is your attention that shifts from your conceptual mind to nonverbal consciousness. Do not expect that your mind can or will give you any information about this nonverbal consciousness. Its presence is not related to the mind. It was there before the formation of your thinking mind. You know it as your attention. This attention is nonverbal, and you are it. Our divisive mind creates conceptual fragmentation for utilitarian needs, and at the same time this mind has divided us from God. This mental misconception has become part of our cultural indoctrination. The need to believe in God and the need to rely on religions are culturally acquired archaic superstitions. With this realization, we abandon mythological beliefs and become aware that we exist as undifferentiated reality.

—

You say that we exist in undifferentiated reality. What does it mean?
It means that there is no division between us and all existence.

—

If, as you say, every idea comes from our cultural collective traditions, what about new and original ideas created by scientists?
New and original scientific ideas are new combinations and interpretations of known ideas that already exist.

—

I am a student of Eastern philosophy. According to the Upanishads, Atman and Brahman are the same. Are you familiar with this statement?
Yes. It is one of the Mahavakyas, which means Great Statements.
That's it. The Self, with a capital *S*—which stands for Atman, a Sanskrit term for nonverbal self—is said to be the only existence. Also, this nonverbal self is said to be identical to Brahman, Sanskrit for the Absolute or Godhood. So the Self and the Absolute are two notions for the only existence there is. In other words, the only existence is Godhood, known to each one of us as our innate Self. This claim is very appealing to my mind. But it is really only a conceptual claim. My instinct tells me that this claim is true, and my emotional mind wants it to be true. And yet my rational mind revolts against it because at every moment of my life my senses are flooding my awareness with an infinite variety of very

convincing forms of physical reality. I want to know how I can possibly understand with total certainty that the Self is the only existence there is.

The way you formulate your question indicates that you want to achieve total certainty with your mind, which you take to be reliable as a source of spiritual knowledge.

Yes, I do. Is it not necessary to have my mental questions answered before spiritual realization?

Yes, it is.

Of course, I would love to have the realization, but at this time my mind demands answers. There must be some purpose in having our mental abilities.

The mind sees the world in fragments, creates its own dilemmas, and then tries to solve them. Look at what your mind does. First it assumes that the self is separate from the rest of the world, and then it wants to understand how it is not separate.

How can I stop my mind from creating these dilemmas?

The mind will stop creating these dilemmas when you understand the role of the mind in our consciousness and why the mind does what it does. The inquiry into the framework of the mind will give you the necessary knowledge. You will also understand the purpose of having mental abilities and mental dilemmas.

What is the framework of the mind according to this inquiry?

Total certainty cannot be achieved with the mind because the mind is an acquired survival tool. The mind is composed of know-how concepts and meant to solve utilitarian challenges of ordinary daily activities. When we realize that conceptual understanding is limited to phenomenal matters, we stop demanding that the mind give us valid information on spiritual matters. The statement in the Upanishads cannot be understood analytically like a conceptual statement. Why? Because it requires a nonverbal realization. This occurs in our consciousness after conceptual knowledge of spirituality has been abandoned. In this state of awareness, we do not perceive existence in fragments but apperceive it as undifferentiated reality. This undifferentiated reality is apperceived by our nonverbal consciousness because nonverbal consciousness itself is an undifferentiated consciousness.

———

I derive a great deal of satisfaction from reading about spiritual enlightenment. You say relying on verbal information is not recommended. Why is that?
What is not recommended is to rely on verbal information as final spiritual knowledge. If you do, you will be confined to your conceptual mind. You will end up having an intellectual understanding of spirituality.
Is my reading a waste of time?
Your reading is useful when it leads to the understanding that relying on verbal information limits you to your thinking mind. Relying on your verbal ability is a mental habit that gives you the false impression that you have achieved spiritual knowledge.
Not relying on my verbal ability gives me a feeling of emptiness.
This feeling of emptiness is the absence of words. This absence of words is your window to nonverbal realization. When you realize that mental knowledge is a bunch of words in your mind, your attention shifts to your nonverbal way of perceiving spirituality, and the feeling of emptiness shifts to the presence of your nonverbal consciousness. Once this takes root, your exclusive reliance on verbal spiritual information will be replaced by nonverbal realization.
How is nonverbal realization different from verbal information?

Nonverbal realization occurs when verbal knowledge is understood to be inadequate and misleading.

———

I am a practicing follower of my religion, and I love to hear about the awareness of nonverbal consciousness. Since it is not a religion, I think that there is no contradiction in this. What do you think?
Awareness of nonverbal consciousness can give you a better understanding of your religion.

———

What is the difference between spiritual understanding and spiritual realization?
Understanding occurs in the thinking mind. Realization is an experience of our innate nonverbal consciousness.

———

Inquiry into my cultural conditioning is very helpful in my spiritual work. There is no established tradition that promotes inquiry into religious teachings in our society.
In most societies there are no established traditions for serious inquiry into the conditioning we receive from our civilization. Scientific inquiry is the exception. Most cultural conditionings tend to be constrictive, and most religions are indoctrinations into mythological beliefs, superstitions, and misinformation. Inquiring into our cultural conditioning can lead to the

elimination of mental constrictions that stand in the way of self-realization.

――

What is God consciousness?
God consciousness is the absence of ideas about God.
How can I feel God consciousness?
God consciousness is felt when ideas about Him are abandoned.
Is God consciousness supernatural?
God consciousness is the consciousness with which you are born.
Why don't I feel God consciousness?
Your consciousness is already filled up with ideas about Him.

――

I like to read the New Testament. I also tried to read the Old Testament but found it without love, dominated by a cold God and full of cruel, ancient stories. I relish the warm, loving words of Christ in the New Testament. Reading books about Mahayana Buddhism, Taoism, Zen, Sufism, Advaita, and Gnosticism helps me understand the words of Christ. But there is one statement I have a hard time fully understanding: It is only through me that you can know God. I am paraphrasing it.

Historians know little about what Christ actually said or what he did for the thirty-three years of his life. The first written accounts of his life appeared more than a century after his death. People who did not know him wrote these stories from oral traditions passed down by many generations. In addition, these stories have been rewritten and retranslated for the last two thousand years. So you cannot take everything in them literally. I would say that much has been lost in translation.

Do you know if other spiritual traditions have said anything like this?

Yes. There are many similar statements. For example, in the Hindu Upanishads, which predate the time of Christ by thousands of years, it says this: It is by knowing the self that God can be known. In other words, it is by knowing what our me is that we can discover what God is. Through the I-inquiry of the Advaita tradition, we discover that our me is the verbal representation of our nonverbal self. It is possible that Christ said something similar: It is through the discovery of what our me is that we can know what God is. This or something like this could have been the original meaning of Christ's statement, but the meaning could have been lost in oral tradition or in translation. There is another possibility. Some historians say that leaders of Christianity intentionally changed the teachings to make their brand of faith unique and exclusive for political reasons. You mentioned that you read Gnostic writings. Gnostics, who were contemporary to Christ, also have a statement like in the Upanishads: When you have gnosis or insight about your own me, you see God.

———

What is the Higgs boson particle, or God particle, that scientists hope to find with their Large Hadron Collider?

This is a question for scientists. Some scientists assume there is a beginning of time. Therefore, they want to find an explanation for the beginning of the world. God particle is a label the news media gave to the smallest known particle. It is assumed to be the basis of all particles, and some scientists think it may help explain the origin of the world. In the future, we will try to discover even smaller particles. This is an unending search in our endeavor to gain utilitarian knowledge needed for our physical survival.

Is there a God particle?

All particles of the world, including us, are God particles.

Oh, I see. Is there a beginning of time or eternal existence?

Both are assumptions that are necessary for scientists to do their research, but both these explanations are fragmented conceptual notions. These assumptions lack logical consistency. For example, the obvious question what was there before time began cannot be answered, and eternity makes time irrelevant.

Do you offer a third alternative?

Awareness of nonverbal consciousness is about spiritual realization, not concepts. Conceptual explanations cannot be relied on for spiritual realization.

What is spiritual realization, and how different is it from scientific understanding?

Scientific understanding is based on conceptual logic and is a product of our assumptions. Spiritual realization is not an assumption. It is a direct acknowledgment of our existing nonverbal consciousness, which can be noticed when our thinking mind is empty of concepts.

What do you mean by direct acknowledgment?

The acknowledgment of your nonverbal consciousness is direct because it does not involve your thinking mind.

All of this is too cryptic. Can you explain?

Scientific verbal assumptions are working hypotheses that change as research progresses. Spiritual realization is unchanging and the same for everyone. It is based on the existing conscious-ness we have at birth. Science is based on evolving thoughts. Spirituality is based on constant innate awareness.

I follow the scientific part, but I do not understand the spiritual part.

The spiritual part needs to be noticed in your awareness, not in your thinking mind. Spiritual awareness is not a mental concept but a state of consciousness that occurs when your thinking mind knows it cannot know. It is void of mental assumptions. It is awareness of the zero-thought-consciousness with which you are born.

Well, it is still too cryptic.

Let's try a different approach. You cannot follow because you are convinced that thinking explains everything you can know. But your basic consciousness does not involve your thinking. For example, you know and you can notice that in you there is what is called *attention*. Don't you?

Yes, I do.

Do you know what this attention is and where it comes from?

Well, no, I do not.

You know that it is there, yes?

Yes.

So you see, not everything that you know depends on your think-ing ability. Now that you are aware of this, you can also notice you have a nonverbal consciousness present in you from birth, which is different from your thinking mind. Essentially you see that you are conscious without your thoughts. Your conscious-ness is not thoughts but innate awareness, devoid of concepts. That is how spiritual realization is different from scientific con-ceptual knowledge, which is based on our thinking mind. Do you follow?

Maybe. I am not sure. I have some idea about what you are saying, but I do not see the importance of it. Really, I feel your statements about nonverbal consciousness are unrealistic or too abstract to make any impact on my understanding of life. I really need . . . I need . . . or I want to know if there is a God. I hope scientists will give us definite proof that God exists. It is important to know about the existence of a God particle. None of the world religions provide proof, but I think scientists can. I read books on religion searching for proof, but I found none. My parents often took me to church, where the preacher used to roar very loudly, saying something like if you do not believe in God you will go to hell when you die. I felt that he himself was afraid of death, so he was trying to convince himself that God would save him. But he never offered any proof that God existed. Early on I understood that most churchgoers were hiding their ignorance of God behind their belief in God.

Belief in God can be used to conceal our ignorance of God. But do you want to know that God exists because you are afraid of death?

Yes. I expected that talking with you would give me the answer.

To know the existence of God, you first need to understand why you think what you think.

I don't follow.

To make it less obscure or, as you say, less cryptic, I will say it differently. You need to become aware that your thinking is an acquired mental conditioning you received from the culture in which you live. You need to understand that your thinking is superimposed on the innate consciousness you are at birth. You are born without this thinking; instead, you are born with your consciousness. Do you understand this?

Yes, I do. It is obvious.
What is not obvious to you is that your thinking is not you and
thoughts are ideas in your mind. Thoughts are assumptions.
You have been indoctrinated into believing that our collective
assumption about the existence of God is reality.
Do you mean that there is no God?
No, I don't mean that. I mean that the idea of God is a mental assumption, a concept. From the way you speak, it appears that
you are chasing the concept of God, thinking it is God. If you
rely on the God you heard about in church or the God particle you learned about from scientists, your attention stays in
your conceptual thinking mind. The proof of God's existence
is not found in conceptual assumptions. You already indicated
you understood that the thinking mind is different from the
consciousness we are at birth. This consciousness is permanent and stable. You can say that it is God-given consciousness. Whereas mental ideas are fashioned by our thinking
ability. They are unstable and subject to different assumptions and interpretations. So put your attention on this stable
innate nonverbal consciousness. Ask yourself who or what is
this awareness to which you refer as *I*. When you find what
this conscious *I* is, you will have the answers to your questions
about the existence or nonexistence of God, about the God
particle, and about death.

**If thoughts are not capable of giving us spiritual knowledge,
then why are our thoughts good?**
Thoughts can be useful for investigating thoughts to show that they
are useless for spiritual knowledge and quite good in practical

matters. Thoughts are acquired utilitarian tools essential for our survival.

———

I would like to add that thoughts can also be very dangerous when misunderstood and misapplied. Our wars are fought because of relying on thoughts as if they are spiritual or political realities. Don't you agree?
Yes, I do. That is why we stress the importance of investigating the makeup and role of thinking.

———

Is there any possibility that one day humanity will understand our own consciousness?
Humanity is a concept in our mind. You are part of humanity, so the question is, can I understand this. Becoming aware of your innate nonverbal consciousness, your nonverbal self, is the answer.

———

In most spiritual or religious groups, there are prescribed practices for followers. Is the I-inquiry considered a practice?
The I-inquiry is not to be practiced. It is a temporary mental procedure for finding our nonverbal consciousness, performed when the need occurs during spiritual seeking.
What about practicing some form of meditation or ritual—is there anything like that?
No, there is nothing like that.

Why?

Think about it. Any form of practice is generated by the need of our mind. If you give in to mental demands, you will go on an unending journey in a conceptual maze that leads further and further away from the nonconceptual innate consciousness you already have. What you need is to become aware of it. Any practice takes you away from it.

How do I become aware of it?

By asking the question *who am I*.

I do ask this question with no success whatsoever.

Unless your asking is urgent, as if your life depended on it, the results won't be forthcoming.

How does one get this type of urgency?

When the disenchantment with mental spiritual knowledge is total.

I did not reach this stage yet. I am still expecting spiritual fulfillment from my mind, and I want to learn how to meditate. What is the best thing to do in my situation?

Continue searching with your mind, knowing that it is the best you can do for now. One of the best activities among mental endeavors is meditation, which can effectively still the mind. If you search and practice meditation as if your life depends on it, you may reach the stage of divine mental disenchantment.

——

Is self-knowledge to know nothing? Can you comment on this?

The statement is correct. However, we must understand that the word knowledge does not mean mental or conceptual knowledge. Self-knowledge refers to nonverbal, nonmental awareness. To know nothing means that the mind knows nothing about nonverbal spiritual realization. The understanding that mentally we know nothing in spiritual matters is the most liberating realization that there is.

So to know nothing does not mean nothing in the absolute sense.

Yes. The mind can have relative utilitarian knowledge. It can know about conceptual information offered to us by our thinking mind. But in this case, it means the mind knows nothing about our nonverbal self. Relative conceptual knowledge of the mind cannot be considered as knowledge of the nonverbal self. Therefore, speaking from the spiritual point of view, mental knowledge is not knowledge.

What happens when we realize that mentally we know nothing in spiritual matters?

This is the end of our mental search and the beginning of spiritual awareness.

———

I read that the mind of an enlightened or realized person is in the state of waking sleep.

This means that the mind does not act under the influence of the ego. Although the ego is still present, it is dormant, inactive, and harmless. Ego is not felt in deep sleep even though it is there. When the mind is understood as an instrument to facilitate practical living and ineffective in spiritual matters, it is as if it goes to sleep while it is awake, thus waking sleep. There is nothing mysterious about it. It is a straightforward description using the analogy of sleep.

———

I have a hard time understanding what the message is in your explanation about nonverbal consciousness. I hear your statements that deny the validity of conceptual claims, but I do not hear any positive instructions to replace them. Am I missing something?

Our nonverbal consciousness is acknowledged as a presence, not as an idea. The acceptance of conceptual information blocks the awareness of our nonverbal consciousness. We use conceptual means to demonstrate the limitation of mental understanding in spiritual matters, but we do not have any instructions for the mind to rely on. The difficulty you have in understanding may be due to your habit of following verbal information that is easily provided by your mind. You believe that the mind is your consciousness.

I experience inner joy from conceptual spirituality. I think I need it.

There are many teachers and books disseminating conceptual spirituality. Positive instructions are given by most religions.

——

I do not understand why there are no statements telling us in positive words what spiritual realization is. I always hear what it is not but never what it is.

If you are told verbally what it is, you will be confined to the meaning of words and remain locked in the mind. When you are informed what it is not, your mind remains open to explore and eventually witness your nonverbal consciousness, which is the innate spiritual awareness you already have. In other words, the negative statement of what it is not addresses our nonverbal consciousness, and the positive statement of what it is addresses our mind.

—

Can thinking stop? I know that I cannot stop thinking with my willpower. But I am told that it occurs to some people, and there are many references to this in spiritual literature. This question has fascinated me since my high school days. I was also told that this is not possible by one of my teachers. I read that it is possible. Could you describe how and why it occurs? And what are the necessary conditions for this to occur?

A stop in thinking refers to the realization of nonverbal consciousness. When thinking stops, our attention stays in nonverbal consciousness. As you said, thinking cannot stop because of our decision. During our waking period, we believe that we have some control over what we think about, but we cannot stop thinking at will. This is because our mind has evolved to be a tool for survival, and if thinking stops, our survival could be at risk. In utilitarian activities, thinking is essential. But it does stop on its own in specific mental conditions. It is common, so we do not pay attention to it. The longest time thinking stops is during dreamless sleep. Also, thoughts come to a stop on their own for brief moments at times of familiarity or mental understanding. For example, when we become familiar with some survival preoccupations or scientific questions or with how to cook a delicious dish, our mind stops thinking about this particular matter and automatically continues to think about some other more pressing issues. That is what normally occurs during our daily mental behavior. There is nothing special about it. At certain times and in certain conditions, some thoughts stop. When the mind knows that our survival is not in jeopardy, thinking stops and we fall asleep. But the mind remains as our vigilant survival warrior. The mind slows down to a point of almost total absence of thinking when there are no survival concerns. This is the time for relaxation. Thinking can become almost absent during concentration on a mantra in meditation. However, thinking is absent during spiritual I-inquiry when we become aware of our nonverbal consciousness.

———

You often emphasize the importance of being aware or being conscious of our existence. What is so important about that?
Being aware of our existence is the same as being aware of our *I am*.
What is so important about the *I am*?
The *I am*, or the awareness of existence, is the gateway to being aware of our nonverbal self.
How does it work?
We are aware of the *I am* without thoughts, which means that this awareness is nonverbal. By paying attention to it, we become aware of our nonverbal self. So being aware of existence shows us that we can be aware nonverbally. Many of us believe that our awareness depends on thinking. This conviction is the main obstacle in spirituality. When we rely on thinking to understand spirituality, what we achieve is verbal understanding. When we become aware of our innate nonverbal consciousness, we become aware of our nonverbal self. The nonverbal self is the *I am*. The *I am* is our divine consciousness. This is the importance of knowing our *I am*.
So if I understand correctly, by being aware of the *I am*, we are aware of our divine origin, yes?
Yes.

So the *I am* is our God consciousness.

Yes, and even the statement in the Bible "I am that I am" can be understood that awareness of the *I am* is the awareness of God consciousness.

―

Why do you say that nonverbal consciousness can be defined by saying what it is not but not what it is? I read spiritual literature written in very positive language, and it gives me a great deal of satisfaction and mental pleasure. I feel deeply that you speak of rudimentary truths, but I am left empty-minded. Why is that?

The "truth," as you called it, is not a mental idea in your mind. It is an acknowledgment of the nonverbal consciousness we are at birth. When you use words to define it, you create a mental label and your attention stays in the mind instead of being in its innate condition, the nonverbal consciousness. Positive language entertains us with concepts, and we remain locked in the mind. When you hear about nonverbal consciousness, you are left without concepts. You are left empty-minded.

What about the Buddhist positive practice of mindfulness that leads to no-mind consciousness?

How can mindfulness be practiced? Mindfulness occurs as the outcome of the realization of no-mind consciousness. No-mind consciousness produces mindfulness. But if you make a mental decision to practice mindfulness, it is an exercise of your mind. Such exercises are positive and beneficial and may produce relief from an overactive mind, which can feel like temporary bliss. Most meditation methods provide similar relief. Nonverbal consciousness can be realized with an empty mind or no-mind, not with positive language or concepts, which are nothing more than our thoughts.

But if we cannot rely on our thoughts, there is nothing else.

This is your assumption. What you said indicates you are convinced that nonverbal consciousness can be defined by our thoughts. When we realize that we cannot verbalize what nonverbal consciousness is, but we can say what it is not, our attention automatically shifts to nonverbal awareness. Nonverbal awareness is not nothing. It is existence. Our attention goes to existence. When verbal knowledge is denied, our attention spontaneously goes to nonverbal awareness, and that nonverbal awareness is our consciousness.

I understand what you are saying. But if nonverbal knowledge is nonverbal, how can it be known with our thoughts? How can we have the feeling of bliss that comes from reading about spiritual truth? How can I experience nonverbal bliss?

The bliss you experience is a sensation within your thinking mind. This experience gives you mental pleasure, a temporary sensation that will whet your appetite for more mental sensations with no end in sight. Awareness of nonverbal consciousness takes place within your innate consciousness without mental sensations. It occurs once and remains with you for the rest of your life.

If mental bliss is temporary, why did you say that it is positive and beneficial?

These experiences may eventually lead to the realization of the nonverbal self.

Is the realization of the nonverbal self an experience that produces pleasurable sensations in our mind?

This realization is not a mental experience. It is an acknowledgment of our solid consciousness as the nonverbal awareness of the *I am*.

You just described nonverbal awareness with positive language by saying what it is.

Yes, I did use the analogy of the *I am* to indicate what the realization of the nonverbal self is like. This analogy is an indirect verbal description. It does not give us the direct awareness of nonverbal consciousness.

What gives us the direct awareness?

It is by saying what it is not that our awareness opens to acknowledge the presence of our nonverbal self.

Can you give me an example of how it happens?

When you realize that the nonverbal self cannot be known with words, your attention automatically becomes open to the presence of our innate nonverbal consciousness.

What is this innate nonverbal consciousness?

I like to label it the holy void.

Why do you label it holy void?

We are born with nonverbal consciousness that is void of thoughts. Consciousness that exists at birth can be called divine or holy, thus holy void.

But holy void is still a verbal description, is it not?

Yes, it is. As long as we talk, we describe it verbally. Verbal description is not awareness of nonverbal consciousness. As you can see, what I said states what it is not. You cannot get away from verbal descriptions unless you state what awareness of nonverbal consciousness is not. So no matter what kind of verbal description is proposed, it automatically generates new mental questions and a need for explanations. That is what we are doing now. The way to stop this is to state what it is not.

But saying what awareness of nonverbal consciousness is not is also part of our mental understanding.

When you go this far in the inquiry, the final condition in which you can dwell is speechlessness.

Awareness of nonverbal consciousness is extremely subtle. I am beginning to realize that instead of trying to pinpoint this subtlety in verbal meanings, as I have been doing so far, I need to shift my attention away from thoughts and look for this subtlety in the part of my consciousness that is not verbal.

Yes.

——

I am confused about the notion of *I*. In some books it is stated that when there is *I* there is bondage and when there is no *I* there is freedom. In other books it says that the realization of the innate *I* is the divine self. These statements seem to be contradictory. Can you explain?

Words do not have one meaning. The specific meaning of *I* is understood in the context in which it is used. The notion of *I* can have a personal meaning of self, me, or ego, but it can also mean the Self, with a capital *S*, which in spiritual literature stands for divine consciousness.

Why is the *I* so important?

The *I* is the first concept used in inquiry. The *who am I* question needs to be addressed before anything else. For example, understanding the role our personal me plays in our mental consciousness leads to the realization of our nonverbal self.

What is the nonverbal self?

It is our divine consciousness with which we are born.

I know that my consciousness is divine. Do I need to do the *who am I* question?

No, you don't. It is for those who do not know this.

———

I am a political science student. Why is there such a strong need for religious beliefs throughout recorded history? Religious belief is equal to the economy as a fundamental sociopolitical force regulating human behavior in times of peace or war. It seems that our mind has a built-in need to harbor beliefs. Understanding belief is essential for our survival. What is the anatomy of belief?

Our innate nonverbal consciousness does not have the need for any belief. Belief is a mental need. Our mind stores concepts, concepts are mental postulations, postulations are assumptions, and assumptions are beliefs in figments of imagination, be they religious or secular. Also, our thinking mind gives us extensive conceptual information about the world for practical and utilitarian purposes necessary for our survival. We believe that this conceptual information is reliable, so we trust our mind. And that is for good reason. The mind is a good steward of our survival needs. The problem starts when we trust the information the mind gives us about abstract matters in the same way as the information about tangible matters. Our mind has an acquired mental ability to create utilitarian concepts based on tangible objects or events. However, concepts about abstract matters are based on imagination and fantasy that can be motivated by fears and wishful thinking. Clear examples are hell, heaven, damnation, resurrection, and salvation in the religious field and political doctrines like capitalism, communism, anarchy, or government rule in the secular field. We do not realize that our thinking mind does not and cannot give us accurate information about intangible matters. We are not always aware of the difference between intangible and tangible matters, so we believe that the mind is reliable in all matters.

So if I understand correctly, this inherent limitation of our mind leads to the creation of religious fantasies that can easily be believed as truths.

Yes. In order to avoid confusing and misleading others, the most appropriate way to describe nonverbal consciousness is to say what it is not.

I was wondering about this aspect of nonverbal consciousness.

When we verbalize what nonverbal consciousness is, we limit our understanding to our conceptual mind. We also create verbal definitions that vary between different social groups. Verbal definitions lead to religious or secular beliefs that unite people with similar beliefs and separate them from groups with different beliefs. As you said, beliefs regulate our behavior during peace and war. They affect our survival.

So our beliefs can be constructive or destructive. Our wars were and still are caused by our religious beliefs. In spite of it, humanity survives, and we continue to live in this condition. I think it is immature and wasteful.

Do not forget that this is the situation with religious beliefs as well as secular beliefs such as political doctrines. Sometimes when conditions change, our constructive beliefs easily become destructive. At other times our destructive beliefs become constructive. We keep juggling. But still, we do not question how detrimental it is to blindly follow our mental beliefs, religious or secular. So the anatomy of belief is a misplaced trust that our culturally conditioned mind gives us absolute and accurate knowledge.

Wouldn't we be better off if humanity could live without these beliefs?

Beliefs can be useful when understood as beliefs. What happens in humanity is the reflection of what happens within each one of us. So the question is, can I live without beliefs. When we understand that belief is misplaced trust in mental information, the need for believing stops. When the burden of mental belief is lifted, we realize that to live with mental beliefs is to live confined to the mind. When we live without those beliefs, our attention stays in nonverbal awareness, our innate divine consciousness.

———

You often speak about nonverbal consciousness. I have given a lot of reflection to this matter, and I must admit that I have no idea what nonverbal consciousness is. The various explanations you give do not help me. I am not a religious person, and I am not a follower of any trendy meditation group. But I am educated enough to think logically, and I can understand and follow complex subjects. I am also a practical and down-to-earth person who believes in common sense. You say nonverbal consciousness cannot be understood mentally, but it can be noticed or realized through experience. I don't have such experiences. At this point I am lost and frustrated. There must be a straightforward approach to this question. Tell me in simple words what this nonverbal consciousness is and how I can get it.

Your own attention is nonverbal consciousness.

How can I get it?

To experience it, what you need to do is to give your attention to your attention. You will instantly be in your nonverbal consciousness.

—

Is mental knowing interpretation or knowledge?
Mental knowing is verbal interpretation.
Do your verbal statements about awareness of nonverbal consciousness carry fixed meanings?
No. My verbal statements carry contextual meanings, like other statements in any discipline that uses language.

—

I am a sociologist. I have one question that has persisted for many years, and I am curious how someone aware of their nonverbal consciousness would answer it. Today and throughout history, the world is in a permanent state of conflict. Why do we continuously kill each other?
The fundamental reason is we mistakenly believe that our thinking is reliable in all matters. Without consent, we unknowingly inherit this misconception from cultural traditions. When we realize that our thoughts are not our consciousness but are an acquired verbal skill, useful to deal with utilitarian matters but useless to give us reliable sociopolitical and religious beliefs, then the tyranny of our agelong indoctrination and misinformation stops. But without this realization there is no personal or social effect.
What does it take to create an effect?
It must start with oneself first. The inquiry into our own consciousness will show us that as civilized people we are subject to a

strong conditioning to believe thinking gives us reliable information about all issues in our lives. This erroneous reliance on the accuracy of our thoughts is the primary cause for being easily indoctrinated by fictitious political and religious beliefs that lead to violence. These beliefs are rarely questioned. It is the questioning of our blind belief in the reliability of our thoughts that will lead to the end of violence.

——

Theists say that God exists, and atheists say that there is no God. Are these statements just verbal attitudes that say the same thing? Are they both wrong or both mean nothing? Yet those who say that God exists and those who say that there is no God are secure and content with their convictions. Why are we so dependent on verbal convictions for our happiness?
Both theists and atheists express opposite verbal beliefs, but both are beliefs. As verbal beliefs they are the same. Verbal information about what exists and what does not exist is not accurate. As you suggest, it means nothing.
How do people who are aware of their nonverbal consciousness deal with this dilemma?
By not taking any verbal position regarding the notion of God.
Why?
Verbal statements limit spiritual understanding.
Do you yourself say that in spiritual matters we should never make any verbal statements?
No. Such a statement would also be a limiting verbal statement.
If so, how can you make any verbal statement or say anything?
We use words that reflect actual states of consciousness in order

to describe them but not to define them or make metaphysical judgments about them.

How does one get mental satisfaction if verbal convictions are eliminated?

If you believe that verbal information gives you valid spiritual information, then you depend on verbal convictions for your happiness. When you understand that verbal knowledge is acquired and resides in our consciousness but is not our consciousness, mental satisfaction from verbal convictions is not needed for your happiness. Freedom from the mental need to know gives you peace.

———

What is a fragmented mind?

By design, the mind's job is to fragment reality into manageable parts called *concepts*. Fragmented minds give us relative utilitarian knowledge.

Who or what gives us absolute knowledge?

Absolute knowledge is a mental concoction.

Then my question is invented or, as you say, concocted by my fragmented and fragmenting mind, yes?

Yes. When you inquire into your consciousness, you realize you are born with nonverbal consciousness. This realization is enlightenment.

———

When we realize that our thoughts cannot say anything meaningful about nonverbal consciousness, what changes in our consciousness?

Our innate nonverbal consciousness never changes. Do you mean a change in the mind composed of thoughts?

Yes, I mean in the mind composed of thoughts.

The acquired mind continues to function the same way. The change occurs in the range of our attention. When you realize that thinking is inherently limited in understanding nonverbal consciousness, your attention does not focus as usual on thinking. Instead, it remains in nonverbal consciousness. What occurs is a shift of your attention from thought-centered to nonverbal awareness. Attention is nonverbal, so when it is no longer attracted by thoughts, the usual place for it to be is in nonverbal consciousness. There is no change in consciousness itself. It is the focus of our attention that shifts.

———

I read that relying on scriptures keeps us in spiritual darkness. If so, can you explain why?

If by reading scriptures you get mental information about spirituality, then you are kept in darkness. Spiritual realization depends on awareness of the nonverbal consciousness we are at birth and is not contained in written words.

———

I just read a book about the history of Advaita. This is my first introduction to the subject. I think of myself as a philosopher. I have rarely been more confused after reading a book.

When we rely on mental knowledge, confusion is inevitable as words carry multiple meanings. Advaita deals with nonverbal matters that are difficult to describe with conceptual language.

Is there a difference between Vedanta and Advaita?

Vedanta uses a conceptual approach to understanding. Advaita uses a nonconceptual approach. Vedanta relies on thinking. Advaita says relying on thinking is an obstacle. Yes, there is a difference, but not many writers point to that difference. Broadly speaking, the term *Vedanta* is applied to Hindu religious philosophy that uses conceptual terminology inspired by nonconceptual Advaita. Because of this verbal association it is often called *Advaita Vedanta.* There are many interpretations of Advaita, of Vedanta, and of Advaita Vedanta that are sometimes contradictory.

When you speak about nonverbal consciousness, is it different from Advaita?

It is the same as the nonconceptual Advaita. The word *Advaita* means nonduality. Nonduality refers to our innate consciousness that is without thoughts; thoughts are dual. Consciousness without thoughts is nonverbal consciousness.

Do concepts play any role?

We use concepts as tools to demonstrate that realization depends on awareness of nonverbal consciousness, not on concepts or mythological beliefs. We act as if our conceptual thinking mind is our consciousness, but our consciousness is nonverbal by birth and precedes the acquisition of our conceptual dual thinking mind.

So if I understand correctly, nonverbal consciousness is our true consciousness, whereas thinking can be called ersatz consciousness. Yes?

Yes, you can call thinking ersatz or imitation consciousness.

How do you become realized?

The direct path to realization is through the inquiry called I-inquiry.

Why is this method direct?

What matters in realization is the thinker, not what the thinker thinks.

How do you do that?

By inquiring who the inquirer is. Know the *I* of the inquirer first.

Why is there a method like the I-inquiry?

There is a method because of the misconception that thinking is our consciousness. We need an intellectual method to extricate ourselves from this faulty intellectual belief. Our thinking prevents us from knowing our nonverbal self.

If we did not have this misconception, how would we know the nonverbal self?

We would know it as our attention.

Does the knowledge of attention lead to the knowledge of the nonverbal self?

Our attention is the nonverbal self.

I see. How do you define the nonverbal self?

It is the ever-present consciousness we are born with.

How can we know this ever-present consciousness?

By paying attention to our attention.

I heard that realization is possible only through a guru.

That is an ancient tradition from the time when most students were illiterate and needed oral instruction. Relying on a guru was a practical need then. Today instruction can be received through multiple means. Relying on a guru stops you from relying on yourself. The guru is a notion in your mind. By having this belief, you stop yourself from inquiring who you are. Instead, your attention is on a guru.

Can you explain the meaning of *not this, not this*? I think it is a translation of the Sanskrit phrase *neti neti*.

Yes, it is. There are two distinct meanings. In Vedanta it is used as a mental exercise in meditation by saying, I am not my body, not my mind, I am not my senses, I am none of these tangible things, I am not this, not this. In Vedanta this mental exercise means that I am divine spirit. In Advaita it refers to undifferentiated reality or what philosophers call *ultimate reality*. It is not possible to define ultimate reality conceptually, so it is said to be *not this, not this*, meaning nothing that we can possibly conceive with our conceptual mind. It is a proposition saying that ultimate reality is not definable.

By ultimate reality, do you mean the Sanskrit concept of Brahman?

Yes.

So I can say that Brahman is *neti neti*, yes?

Yes. It means that Brahman is not definable.

I see. How would you describe awareness of nonverbal consciousness?

It cannot be described verbally but can be realized as the consciousness with which we are born. Verbal description stops inquiry and deflects our attention away from nonverbal awareness.

——

I would like to discuss the Advaita notion of Atman, which is Sanskrit for *Self.* Is there a notion equivalent to Atman in Western philosophical traditions?

Atman means the personal and universal consciousness combined in one word. Usually the label of *Higher Self* or *Self with a capital* S is used. I call it nonverbal self. In the West there is no translation of Atman with one word. We can come close with words like spirit, Holy Ghost, or soul.

I have been reading books on spirituality and religion for over forty years. Sometimes the more I read, the more I get

confused. Lately, after reading books on Advaita, I became aware that there is a strong emphasis on the need to know the Higher Self, which you call nonverbal self. What is so important about the nonverbal self?

Explanations have little meaning without first knowing who the seeker is. You said that sometimes the more you read the more you get confused. Verbal explanations will not satisfy us for long, maybe a little bit initially, but eventually we will have to come to grips with knowing who we are. And that knowledge is possible when we discover our nonverbal self.

Why do you say "discover" it?

It feels like a discovery at first. Most of us usually think of it as a concept, such as me, myself, I am so-and-so, I am somebody. Our attention goes primarily to thoughts, which we consider to be ours. We do not realize that thoughts are acquired from our culture. Our fundamental consciousness is without cultural conditioning and empty of mental meaning. We do not notice it, but this emptiness is our solid nonverbal consciousness with which we are born. This thought-free consciousness is also called the *empty mind* or the *nonverbal self.* It is your familiar and ordinary attention that you take for granted.

Is my attention that I take for granted supposed to be my non-verbal self?

Yes. Both attention and the nonverbal self are labels for nonverbal consciousness.

You mean that I can be aware of my nonverbal self simply by being aware of my attention?

Yes. But this is another verbal explanation. You realize your nonverbal self when you stop relying on verbal information and face this mental emptiness that is your intrinsic, innate consciousness.

How do I face this innate mental emptiness and stop relying on verbal information?

Our habit of relying on thinking has been cultivated since childhood. Thinking is a useful tool for our survival but not for awareness of our nonverbal consciousness. There comes a time when we become fed up with mental information. At this point you may become desperate. When this happens, your attention may turn away from everything and everyone you have known and focus on the fundamental question of what is this consciousness in me. Who or what is this conscious *I*? This question will open a vast world of nonverbal awareness, which at first appears like emptiness from the point of view of our habitual thinking. When your consciousness is empty of mental meaning, you apperceive your nonverbal consciousness. Then reliance on verbal meaning for nonverbal matters will stop.

I have been fed up with verbal explanations for years now. Why do most books talk about mental understanding? None of these books tell me how to know the nonverbal self.

What you seek is not found in books or in someone else's explanations. It is a question of where your attention goes.

What do you mean by where the attention goes?

Your attention can focus on your thoughts or on your nonverbal consciousness.

And what is nonverbal consciousness?

Your first question about the nonverbal self is the fundamental concern that leads to the awareness of our nonverbal consciousness. The nonverbal revolves around our awareness of the nonverbal self.

I see. So I have questions about nonverbal consciousness. For example, what is the meaning of the *I am*? There is a Christian

Church of the *I Am*. Christ said, "Before Abraham was, I am." In the Old Testament God's name is said to be "I am that I am." And the notion of *I am* is frequently mentioned in spiritual writings. What is so important about the *I am*? I often read about it and never fully understood why knowing that I exist is so important.

Knowing *I exist* or *I am* engages our attention. Our ordinary, everyday, unassuming attention is nonverbal consciousness. Awareness of the *I am* is the gateway to the realization of our nonverbal self. The *I am* is a way of realizing that there is a consciousness independent from cultural mental conditioning. That consciousness is the divine consciousness we are at birth. That is the importance of knowing about the presence of the *I am*. Christ's statement "Before Abraham was, I am" can mean that divine consciousness existed before creation. The biblical statement that God's name is "I am that I am" can be understood as to know the *I am* is to know God.

I see. I have tried to use the *who am I* question in my meditation without much result. What is the best way to do it?

The *who am I* inquiry is not for meditation. Do you use it like a mantra?

No, not like a mantra. I do it when I am in a relaxed, meditative mood.

This question is more effective when you genuinely need to know or, better, when you are desperate to know. Your casual approach keeps you confined in the intellect. You do it out of a mental concern because you read or heard about it. Maybe you do not experience a genuine need.

How can I experience the need? As I said, I am already fed up with mental explanations. I want more than that.

Evidently your intellect needs more answers. When you exhaust

your questions, the *who am I* inquiry occurs in you spontaneously. You do not need to formulate it in your mind.

So that means my questions are beneficial in the long run.

Yes, they are. It is a useful inquiry that is bound to produce results.

Why does the *I* play such an important role in inquiry?

Inquiry deals with the *I* first because it is considered a direct approach. The main reason inquiry of the *I* is direct is that the *I* is
the common denominator to every thought.

**Can you explain the concept of the *I* being a common denomi-
nator to every thought?**

Without the presence of *I*, thinking is not possible. The *I* is the root
cause of every thought. If you pay attention, you can notice that
the *I* is present no matter what you think and as long as you
think.

**Is that why the *I* plays such a crucial role in Advaita and why the
Upanishads keep clamoring that without knowing the self,
nothing else can be known?**

Yes. And who knows this?

I do.

You see. Your *I* is always present.

**Then knowing the self should be the priority of our attention.
How can we know the self? I do not mean the verbal self, like
me or myself or I am so-and-so. These are mental concepts.
My consciousness is independent of my thinking. Yes?**

Yes. When you are aware of this, you do not need to search to know
the self. You already know it. Strictly speaking, this awareness,
which is nothing else but our innate attention, is the nonverbal
self.

**Is this innate attention, which is the same as our awareness of
the nonverbal self, what the Upanishads refer to as Atman?**

Yes.

I read in an Advaita book that since the only existence is Atman and there are no objects, thoughts cannot arise at all because thoughts can function only when there are objects. Can you explain what that means?

This is an accurate description of what happens to our thoughts after the realization of Atman, which I call nonverbal self. Our thoughts divide the world into segments called objects, but we are not our thoughts. To understand this statement, we need to realize that our thinking ability is an acquired survival skill functioning in consciousness, but it is not our consciousness.

This is very difficult to understand.

The statement that there are no objects cannot be understood correctly if we view the world through the usual conceptual means of our mind, meaning through the thinking process. However, this statement can be understood after you uncover the nonverbal self.

That is my dilemma. I say to myself that there are objects because I see them.

Listen. These objects are seen as separate entities because our divisive utilitarian mind interprets undifferentiated reality as multiple objects for survival needs. When this same world is seen after our nonverbal self is realized, those objects are understood not as separate but as part of undifferentiated reality. And undifferentiated reality itself is understood not as an objective world but as consciousness. There are no separate objects. There is nothing but consciousness. When this is grasped, this statement is accepted as an obvious and correct description of our nonverbal awareness.

What do I need to do to grasp this?

When you use thoughts to understand the verbal meaning of this statement, you keep your attention locked in the conceptual mind. What you get from this is more concepts or more ideas that give you short-lived understanding. Instead, turn your attention to who wants to understand. This will lead you to your nonverbal self.

How do I do that?

Ask yourself who wants to grasp. Do not expect a verbal answer. When your attention acknowledges your innate nonverbal consciousness, you have realized your nonverbal self.

I have often asked *who am I* or who wants this or that, and my answer is always I do not know.

It is your mind that says I do not know. This is a verbal answer. You do not want a verbal answer. Ask who knows that your mind does not know. Keep your attention on the consciousness that knows this. This consciousness is nonverbal. The mind cannot label it. When you acknowledge the presence of this nonverbal consciousness, you realize that this is your nonverbal self. The realization of nonverbal self is the realization of undifferentiated reality where there are no objects and no need for thinking. Said succinctly, to understand this, first find this consciousness you refer to as *I*.

——

What is the difference between monotheism and nonduality or Advaita?

Monotheism means that there is one God, not many gods. Nonduality means that there is nothing else but God.

It is easy to understand and visualize one God, but I cannot quite do the same with nonduality. I am very taken by nonduality,

and I would like to understand it or visualize it. I know that at the moment I have an intellectual notion of it. I still see the world, God, and us as separate from each other.

Initially, mental visualization is helpful. But the awareness of non-duality occurs for good when we are in touch with our nonverbal consciousness and know that our consciousness is divine. Then we perceive God, the world, and us as one and the same. This is possible when you investigate who you are. Once you know that your consciousness is divine, you no longer look at God and the world through your fragmenting thinking mind. Instead, you perceive the undifferentiated reality, which is the same as seeing that everything is Godhood—better yet, that there is nothing but Godhood.

But my mind already tells me that I am a divine creation in God's nature. All I need now is to understand and perceive or mentally visualize that everything is Godhood. I still see separation everywhere. Am I the only one like that? I hope not.

No. Your concern is as old as civilization. This difficulty is a classic question that has been discussed for thousands of years, long before the birth of Christ. There is an ancient saying that can be helpful in creating a preliminary mental understanding. So listen attentively. It contains a subtle meaning. It goes like this: Godhood appears separate from the world and us in the same way that a rope appears as a snake without undergoing any change.

—

Empty mind has a prominent place in Advaita. What other disciplines emphasize the importance of empty mind?

Empty mind occurs regularly in human consciousness. There is reference to it under different labels in many traditions. **So it is not unique to Advaita.** No, it is not. What is different and unique is how it is explained. In many traditions the empty mind is cloaked in esoteric terms. In Advaita the language is direct.

——

What is the role of imagination?
Imagination is a tool of the mind. Imagination understood as imagination is beneficial for our survival. Our know-how, our sciences, and our relationships depend on it. However, imagination understood as absolute truth can be detrimental. When this occurs, it can lead to activities contrary to survival.

——

Philosophy is based on reason. I started reading philosophy because I was convinced philosophy replaces religion. It does not. My metaphysical malaise persists.
Philosophy and religion rely on conceptual information available in the mind. The mind stores information obtained from our cultural traditions. Those traditions are verbal. Metaphysical malaise stops when we realize that we are not our verbal mind. We are born with nonverbal consciousness. We use reason in self-inquiry to realize nonverbal consciousness, not to define concepts. Nonverbal consciousness is called by many names, such as *inner light, thought-free awareness, nonverbal attention,* and *undifferentiated consciousness.* Buddhists call it *no-mind* or *emptiness.* Hindus call it *not this, not this* or *silence.* Christians

call it *divine unknowing* or *holy mystery*. I call it *holy void*. There are many ways of labeling it. Poetic Sufi or paradoxical Zen and Tao labeling is appropriate too. Relying on precise definitions of concepts keeps our attention in the mind. The realization of nonverbal consciousness does not require concepts. It is not a mental event.

———

Is there life, intelligent life, in the universe outside of planet Earth?
This is a question for astrobiologists.
I am an astrobiologist. I want to know if with your awareness you think it is possible.
I think it is possible.

———

I heard that there is spirituality without God. What does it mean?
God-realization occurs without believing in God.
How is this possible?
Believing occurs in the mind. Realization occurs in nonverbal consciousness.
Are we not born with the mind too?
We are born with an ability to have a thinking mind, but we are born without thoughts. The thinking mind is a culturally acquired tool for survival. The thinking mind is not our consciousness.

———

Brainwashing is an accepted form of educating society in secular and religious beliefs. For better or worse, we have not yet found a way of conditioning society without relying on mental beliefs. Is learning about nonverbal consciousness also brainwashing?

Brainwashing occurs in the thinking mind. Through inquiry we realize that we are not the mind but are nonverbal consciousness by birth. And nonverbal consciousness cannot be brainwashed.

———

If our mind cannot know who I am, why ask?

We ask to realize that the mind cannot know.

———

Our mind fragments reality into concepts. Can concepts give spiritual realization?

The ability to fragment reality into concepts is necessary to function in a complex phenomenal environment. This ability, however, cannot give spiritual realization.

Why?

Spiritual realization is non-differentiated consciousness, the opposite of fragmented consciousness of the mind.

———

Why does the I-inquiry lead to mental void?

The I-inquiry leads to a mental void because the mind does not know what the *I* is.

What is nonverbal awareness, and how is it related to our thoughts?

Nonverbal consciousness is the one you have at birth, and it is with you now too. It is present prior to the mental cultural conditioning that you receive for many years after you are born. Nonverbal consciousness is empty of mental meaning. Thoughts are composed of mental meaning. During waking hours we primarily give our attention to our thoughts, which we take to be our consciousness. We do not realize that thoughts are in our consciousness, but they are not consciousness. We fail to notice that our awareness is present without thoughts. Inquiry gives us the opportunity to peek into our thought-free consciousness. Once this occurs, we realize that the core of our consciousness is nonverbal, in the same state as it was at birth. This realization gives us a broader awareness of our consciousness. We realize that our nonverbal consciousness is the same as the nonverbal consciousness in deep sleep. When we keep our attention in this nonverbal consciousness, we experience the same state of contentment that exists in deep sleep. The outcome of this realization is that our thinking process occurs while it is based in the sleeplike contentment of nonverbal consciousness.

If our thinking occurs in sleeplike contentment, is this any different from the immature and irresponsible thinking of very young children?

Your statement refers to the undeveloped intellect in children. When we act from nonverbal consciousness as adults with fully developed intellects, we function responsibly. In the sleeplike nonverbal consciousness, the ego is present but inactive or dormant. If you do not like the label *sleeplike consciousness*, you could call it *nonmental consciousness*. In adults, thinking overshadows this nonmental consciousness, but it is present in us. Pay attention to your attention. Our attention is this nonverbal consciousness.

Can you explain why we think at all?

The knowledge that we are mortal is the main cause of the type of thinking we do. Utilitarian thinking is about physical survival, and religious thinking is about spiritual survival. Our acquired thinking mind is a tool for survival. We think in order to survive.

Do we have free will?

Did you use free will to be born? Our fragmenting mind creates all sorts of imaginary concepts. Free will is one of them.

Today and throughout history our political and religious leaders utilize misinformation to achieve their goals. Why are we so easily fooled by misinformation? Why are we so gullible?

The belief that thinking and consciousness are the same is the fundamental misinformation we inherit from our civilization. When we are subject to this misinformation, other types of misinformation are easily accepted. When you understand that thinking is not consciousness, you can no longer be fooled.

Is there any value in thinking?

Do you mean the value of thinking in general or with awareness of our nonverbal consciousness?

I would like to hear your take on both. In schools we are trained to think logically. We are told that thinking is the most valuable ability we have to deal with situations and to understand our role as humans living in this world. It does not appear that it always works very well. We are destroying the only planet we have to live on, and we have not found a better home yet in this vast universe. Our religions are supposed to help, but instead they cause conflicts that they justify with ill-conceived sectarian dogmas. We invent new political, social, or economic systems that do not perform any better than religions. History is full of bleak examples. I think that our thinking is to be blamed.

Thinking is based on the dichotomy of ideas. In the phenomenal world, dichotomy is the norm. For every bleak example you cite, a positive example could be cited too. The phenomenal world continuously seeks balance. We have not destroyed our planet yet. Knowing how dangerous thinking can be should encourage us to think constructively. But no matter how much positive thinking we do, the negative thinking will still be there. In general, thinking is essential for human civilization in this phenomenal world. Thinking, however, is the main obstacle to the realization of our nonverbal self, and at the same time we rely on thinking to identify obstacles during I-inquiry. Most of us consider thinking to be our main consciousness. But thinking prevents us from noticing that our fundamental consciousness is without thoughts. The I-inquiry demonstrates how thinking dominates our knowledge and how we can extricate ourselves from that dominance. We seek awareness of our nonverbal consciousness and consider thinking as a tool to facilitate this search.

―――

If we can't see our nonverbal self with our mind because the nonverbal self is nonverbal consciousness, then how do we see it and how do we know about it?

This question is asked by a mind not convinced that it cannot see the nonverbal self. That's why it is still asking. When the mind knows and is convinced it cannot see the nonverbal self, it realizes that the reason the nonverbal self cannot be seen is because the nonverbal self makes seeing possible.

―――

Why are there so many different philosophical, psychological, and religious systems that often contradict each other? Our knowledge of mind and consciousness is confusing.

You refer to conceptual knowledge based on mental conditioning we receive from our civilization, an accumulation of information in the form of words in our mind. Words or ideas have many contradictory meanings that change with time and in different social groups. Words can easily cause confusion. These acquired notions are not our consciousness. Our consciousness is nonverbal and empty of mental conditioning. Our nonverbal consciousness is permanent and does not undergo any change from the time of our birth.

I do not understand. I do not even know what nonverbal consciousness is.

When you say, "I do not know," you are in nonverbal consciousness. You do not notice it because your thoughts and words usurp your attention. You do this out of habit.

I don't follow.

Listen carefully. To say "I do not know" means you do not know words that describe nonverbal consciousness. That is right because nonverbal consciousness cannot be described or defined by words. You cannot mentally know nonverbal consciousness. And you do not need to know it. You need to notice it with your attention, not with your thoughts. In other words, nonverbal consciousness is always present. You do not need to seek it. You notice it by shifting your attention from words to the self who does not know. The one who does not know is nonverbal consciousness, your nonverbal self. The moment you know, you are back in the conceptual conditioned mind.

That is simple.

——

I read that it is possible to stop thinking. I am thinking all the time, and I can't stop it. I will graduate from high school this summer, and I do not know what I will do afterward.

Are you aware of your attention?

Yes.

Good. Attention is the key to understanding how thinking can stop. We do not notice our attention easily because we are born with it. Attention is another word for the self, and it is through this mute attention that we can become aware of what the thoughts are doing and if they can come to a stop. When you try to stop thinking, the trying itself adds more thinking, so you have the opposite effect. When thinking is in progress, we have no control over it. But we have control over our attention. A good question is if thinking stops on its own during deep sleep, why not during waking hours. And indeed, that is what happens in the condition known as the awareness of nonverbal consciousness. In nonverbal consciousness, thinking stops by itself while we are awake. So the question is what is nonverbal consciousness, and how do we get it. Yes?

Yes.

Our attention is our nonverbal consciousness. If your attention stays on your attention, there are no thoughts and you are awake. That is how you know that thoughts can stop.

I do that often, but I never pay attention to it.

Out of habit you think that your attention and your thoughts are the same. You can give your attention to your thoughts, but the attention itself is not a thought. You are in control of your attention. So use that control.

Okay. My attention stays on my attention only for a moment.

Even if you notice it for a moment, this realization will always stay with you. Knowing you have this ability is important. You do not need to stay there all the time. Practical living demands your attention for all sorts of things. But if you pay attention, you will notice that during waking hours we are often in our nonverbal attention without being conscious of it. We continuously shift between nonverbal attention and thinking. Our attention bounces between thought-free and thought-present states. So since you are in control of your attention, you can choose where you want to be. When you become more and more conscious of your attention, it will not matter if there are thoughts or no thoughts. You will be in a state similar to deep sleep while you are awake. In this state you will notice that at times your attention will be with thoughts because life demands it, and at other times your attention stays in nonverbal consciousness where thoughts are absent.

But if the thoughts stop when my attention is on the attention, it happens for only a brief moment. After that the thoughts come back.

What matters is to be aware of it. It is brief now because you have not yet developed your skill to pay attention to your attention.

What is the benefit of having this skill?

The same benefit you have from deep sleep.

I do not want to be in a sleeplike state. I am still in high school. I need my mind wide awake.

The purpose of being in the nonverbal state is to be wide awake with a feeling of well-being due to the absence of thoughts, like the one you have in deep sleep.

Oh, that is cool. Then how can I get this?

You establish the new habit of managing your attention.

How?

Whenever you remember or feel like it, or in your spare time, ask yourself who or what is this attention. After repeated attempts, when you become familiar with it, you will notice that this attention is present all the time in everything you do or think. You will learn that your attention and your me are one and the same. When you know that, you consciously participate with your attention in things that interest you. And when you want to rest in the nonverbal state, you can put your attention on the attention itself. You can do it for a brief moment or as often and as long as you want. Remember, your attention is nonverbal. In this state there is no thinking. So knowing this, you can avoid unwanted thoughts and create a feeling of well-being. Remember, you are in charge of your attention.

Why don't they teach this in school?

If you learn this yourself, you may one day teach this to others.
So all I have to do is pay attention to my attention?
Yes.

———

Many decades ago, I was an avid reader of spiritual books. I no
longer do that. Now I listen. This way I can hear the essence
of things much, much better. I would like to hear what you
think about what I think of the awareness of nonverbal consciousness. I am in awe of how the awareness of nonverbal
consciousness is simple and ordinary. From complex, so-
phisticated questions about various enlightenments and
different approaches to self-knowledge emerges the awareness that realization is simply to be conscious of our innate
attention.
Yes. I agree.

———

**If our attention is nonverbal and you say that it is our nonverbal
self, is it what you call holy void?**
Yes. These are different labels for the same nonverbal awareness we
have at birth.
**I am aware of my attention, but I do not feel that it is my non-
verbal self. For me, attention is only a concept in my mind.
What do I miss?**
Attention can also be a mental concept. But when you realize you
were born with this attention and your conceptual mind was
developed later, you become aware that your innate consciousness is nonverbal and has little in common with the concepts

of your mind. That awareness is the same as the nonverbal self, the holy void. It cannot be anything else. You were born with it. When you realize this, your attention will automatically go to rest in this holy void. Ask yourself where your attention comes from. Find this out.

———

Many established traditional religions advocate the power of belief. What is the power of belief?
It can be helpful to some people. But essentially, religious belief is a placebo cure for mental insecurity caused by faulty thinking.
What do you mean by faulty thinking?
It is the flawed and misleading belief that thinking gives us valid information about our consciousness.
How powerful is the belief that thinking is our consciousness?
The power of this belief is enormous until we realize that thinking is not the consciousness we have at birth but is an acquired practical mental utensil.

———

Does enlightenment make people impervious to pain?
This is another misconception that occurs when we rely on cultural indoctrination based on mythological creeds. When we are under the sway of unverifiable beliefs based on mental fabrications, we have a propensity to believe in miracles and supernatural or paranormal events, such as walking on water, resurrection or ascension, extraordinary appearances or heavenly visions, and the like. So being impervious to pain is one of those figments of imagination we attribute to special people. To feel pain

is necessary to optimize our survival chances. However, there are Hindu yogis, Buddhist monks, and others who have what are called supernatural powers to control pain or even stop or slow down heartbeats and breathing. This is a form of mental control over the body, akin to self-hypnosis or an extreme mental self-persuasion. Is this enlightenment? Spiritual enlightenment is not related to mental or physical achievements. So first find out what enlightenment is before what it does.

———

When I hear you speak about the need to realize that we are not our thoughts, I am reminded of what psychologists call *multiple personalities*. Is the realization that I am not my thoughts and thoughts are not my consciousness a form of multiple personalities syndrome?

No. You went in the wrong direction in your analysis. Listen carefully. The belief that thoughts are our consciousness leads to the condition called multiple personalities. This belief keeps most of us in what could be called a permanent state of mild multiple personalities syndrome. Why? How often do we define or represent ourselves differently to different people in different circumstances. We have learned this in our childhood by behaving quite differently with our parents than with our friends. This is possible because we believe we are our thoughts, which we use to hide or create different realities. In some specific conditions, this common tendency can develop into full-blown multiple personality syndrome.

Oh, I see. It's exactly the opposite of what I thought.

Yes, it is. Do you want to hear about other ramifications stemming from the belief that we are our thoughts?

Yes.
Identification with our thoughts creates the false conviction that thinking gives us absolute and reliable truth. This, in turn, leads to an unconditional interpretation of secular laws and religious scriptures. An absolutist interpretation can lead to patriotic or religious zeal on one hand and on the other hand to fanatical behavior that can lead to secular or religious terrorism.

Is this the origin of evil?
Evil stems from the unquestioned belief that we are our thoughts.

I am afraid of the nonverbal self because you say that it is nonpersonal. I already have low self-esteem. I fear that I will become less of a person.
What you say shows that you have a strong personality. Personality is necessary in our practical day-to-day living. It is the role of our thinking mind to create and maintain a personality that stays with us during our lifetime. However, to become mature spiritually, we need to be conscious of our innate nonpersonal awareness, which is our nonverbal self. When this occurs, we become more conscious as a person, not less.

Is there any teaching in the awareness of nonverbal consciousness? The reason I am asking is because I find an inordinate amount of verbal contradictions. I like logic and intellectual precision, but I also accept that life is not always logical and certainly not precise. And because of it, life is intriguing and often entertaining. Although I do not mind being

entertained by contradictions, I would like to have a sensible understanding even if this understanding is a paradox.
Conceptually, awareness of nonverbal consciousness is not a teaching. If it were, it would add more misconceptions to our already confused and heavily conditioned conceptual minds. Paradoxically, we use conceptual ideas to demonstrate that our consciousness is nonconceptual, which accounts for the inordinate amount of verbal contradictions. And pragmatically, in spite of paradoxes and verbal contradictions, the realization of nonverbal consciousness is enlightenment.

————

There are no spiritual teachings. Spiritual teachings are figments of the imagination of immature minds of people who do not know what to do with their thoughts. They invent mythological stories to give meaning to a world they do not understand. And in the process, they gain social importance, become leaders, and exploit naïve people.
What you are saying is applicable to conceptual teachings. Awareness of our nonverbal consciousness is not a conceptual teaching. The I-inquiry demonstrates the shortcomings of conceptual teachings based on verbal knowledge limited to our culturally conditioned mind. Present within the individual, nonverbal consciousness does not require beliefs or mythologies. It is a matter of apperception, not imagination.

————

The book *The Philosophy of As If* by Hans Vaihinger gave me a great deal of mental clarity. After reading it I realized that

my guru teaches conceptual Vedanta. I would like to graduate to awareness of nonverbal consciousness. Can having read this book help me do this? Do you know the book?

Yes, I do. *The Philosophy of As If* explains that our verbal knowledge can be considered as if true for convenience and practical reasons, but not as absolute truth. Awareness of the limitations of our mental knowledge is indispensable in the realization of our nonverbal consciousness.

———

What is death? Or, let me rephrase my question: How do you define the notion of death?

Intellectually it can be defined as a fragmented notion.

Do you mean that death is a mental concept?

Yes. The notion of death is a mental way to interpret the occurrence of death, but the occurrence itself cannot be interpreted because it is part of undifferentiated existence.

It is too esoteric to follow. I need to understand what you mean by undifferentiated existence.

Your question about the notion of death is really a question about the mental labeling of death. This is a conversation about the meaning of words. We can discuss the meaning of undifferentiated existence. Listen carefully. The mind perceives existence by fragmenting it into separate elements called objects, which are concepts. Without fragmentation, existence is nondifferentiated. Therefore, the notion of death is a fragmented perception of undifferentiated existence. What is certain about death is that we know about it as a fragmented concept. In other words, our mind can know the idea of death but nothing else. Does this answer your question?

Yes, it does. So the same reasoning is applicable to all mental concepts like birth, karma or destiny, free will or God's will, time and space, the universe at large, the universe within, and so on. Concepts are fragmented interpretations of un-differentiated existence. Apart from mental concepts, our mind knows nothing else about existence.

Yes. This realization tells you that our thinking conceptual mind is a good instrument to deal with utilitarian matters where frag-mented conceptual information is needed. But it is not capable of understanding matters of undifferentiated existence.

How do we understand existence?

It can be realized directly by being in touch with nonmental con-sciousness. It is present at birth, prior to the development of the thinking mind.

How does one get in touch with nonmental consciousness?

The inquiry of who you are shows that you are not a thinking mind, but the thinking mind is in your nonmental consciousness.

You mean that this is done through the I-inquiry?

Yes.

———

Is there free will? I mean, do we have free will? One teacher says that there is God's will, not our personal will. This means everything is predetermined, so there is no free will. How do you deal with this question?

The statement that there is God's will is a typical answer from most religions. With awareness of nonverbal consciousness, the question of free will is not answered conceptually. Conceptual answers are manufactured by our thinking mind. If accepted, we lock ourselves in the confines of our mind. To say there is no free will or there is free will or there is God's will indicates that we rely on mental knowledge. This wallowing in mental notions fascinates our mind. The mind can invent an infinite amount of conceptual situations. For example, it also can say that our belief in free will is in itself predetermined. This type of mental paradox challenges our need to make verbal sense out of mental fictions. The mind creates its own mental scenarios with obstacles and enjoys solving them. That is how our cultural myths are created. This is a form of intellectual entertainment. Mental judgments of this type do not give us any valid information about the world we live in.

Do you say anything about free will?
The question of free will is made up by the mind. The need to have a mental answer to a fictitious mental question indicates that we consider our thinking mind as our consciousness. We have not realized that our consciousness is not of the mind. Therefore, to answer your question, we have to first know who creates the question about free will.

—

When I put my attention on my attention, what am I supposed to experience?
Your divine consciousness as holy void.
Oh yes. I have that.

—

Why is divine consciousness likened to a holy void?
To avoid associating the divine with acquired verbal notions.
Why would that be wrong?

It is misleading to think that the divine is a known mental concept.
So void means void of mental concepts, yes?
Yes.
It seems to me that when we no longer rely on verbal concepts, our realization is the awareness of this holy void present in our life at all times. This realization is nothing more than an awareness of it as our innate consciousness.
Yes.

———

When I was studying my religion, I always had a feeling of achievement. When I hear about awareness of nonverbal consciousness, I often feel lost, and I question why I am confused. Since I am confused, I must miss something fundamental. What is that? Do you follow what I am saying?
I follow. And here is a possible reason. Your religion requires verbal understanding in your mind, but here verbal understanding is not the goal. The goal is the empirical experience of our nonverbal consciousness. This experience is not the usual thinking experience. It is an apperception of what already exists. It is more the ability to notice than to understand mentally. Conceptual knowledge gives you the feeling of achievement in the mind. Nonverbal realization gives you a feeling of awe in your being.
So I should not expect any mental feelings of achievement.
Continue questioning, probing, and inquiring. The mental feeling of achievement stops inquiry and is contrary to nonverbal realization.
What is nonverbal realization?
It is the awareness of our innate nonverbal consciousness.

—

After hearing about the awareness of our nonverbal consciousness, what kind of understanding is one supposed to have? I often have more questions than answers. Why is that?

There are no conceptual answers. The best question to ask yourself is who you really are.

—

I made a short list of various types of consciousness referred to in literature. There is divine, universal, mental, absolute, personal, verbal, nonverbal, conceptual, nonconceptual consciousness, and more. I have a fairly analytical mind and like to have a clear intellectual understanding. I read that consciousness is obvious. It is not obvious to me. It is confusing. I would like to know what consciousness is.

The fundamental question is what is consciousness. How would you like to approach this question? Would you like an analytical inquiry into verbal definitions of the word consciousness, or would you prefer a direct answer?

I prefer a direct answer. I have done the analysis many times and I still do not know what consciousness is.

So you have an important and useful realization that to understand verbal definitions does not give you knowledge of what consciousness is.

Why is it important and useful?

Now you know the limitation of verbal definitions, so you are ready to look in a different area of your awareness. Verbal understanding keeps you in the mind. So in addition to your intellectual understanding, you can learn about the presence of consciousness within you.

That is right. I want to experience it. So what is this direct answer?

Instead of putting your attention on the word consciousness as you have been doing so far, put your attention on the attention itself. You are this attention. This attention is consciousness.

———

Why is conceptual knowledge not accepted as true in understanding nonverbal consciousness?

The knowledge of nonverbal consciousness is the result of nonverbal realization, referred to as insight. Our practical, mundane, and scientific knowledge is based on the way our mind functions. The mind perceives by dividing our world into manageable fragments called objects. Our consciousness uses the mind as the instrument to do this. However, this mind is not our consciousness but is in our consciousness. Our consciousness cannot be perceived by the mind because consciousness is not an object. Consciousness makes mental perceptions possible. Therefore, conceptual knowledge cannot be used as valid information about our consciousness.

But aren't you using conceptual mental language to talk about consciousness?

To talk about it we have to use conceptual means. Communication takes place with the help of the intellect, which is composed of concepts. That is as far as we can go conceptually. Nonverbal attention is needed to be aware of our nonverbal consciousness, which is present from the time of our birth. We are born with our nonverbal attention. We are born without thoughts. We do not easily notice this nonverbal attention because our attention is usurped by utilitarian conceptual thoughts. This habit stops with the discovery of the presence of our innate consciousness through the I-inquiry process. If conceptual or verbal means are used, this leads to the formation of philosophical doctrines and religious dogmas that eventually end up in the arsenal of mythological distortions stored in the collective memory of our civilization.

But what advantage is there to knowing about our nonverbal consciousness?

Realization of nonverbal consciousness frees you from the limitations of conceptual understanding.

——

I believe that the way we are, the way nature or God made us, is complete and perfect. So there must be a way to know the Self, with a capital S, without resorting to any method devised by the intellect.

Yes. The direct way to know the self is to be aware of our ever-present attention. Our nonverbal attention is the self.

——

Mystics say that surrendering the ego or mind is the easiest and the ultimate way to know the Divine. With awareness of nonverbal consciousness, is there a need for surrender?

We are born with divine nonverbal consciousness, and the ego or mind are tools for survival. When you realize this, the ego or mind need not be surrendered.

——

If I understand correctly, any conceptual statement about non-mental realization is incorrect because it originates from a mental understanding.

Yes.

I read the statement that there is no me. Is this not a conceptual statement?

Yes, it is. Many authors use a mental approach and do not make a distinction between conceptual understanding and nonverbal realization.

So this statement comes from conceptual writings on spirituality, yes?

Yes.

How do you define conceptual spirituality?

In conceptual spirituality you find mental answers to mental questions fabricated by the mind.

Oh, I see. Do you teach conceptual spirituality?

I like to talk about nonverbal consciousness.

How do you address the idea of me?

The me exists as a mental notion and is the same as the notion of ego. The me is the mental representation of our nonverbal self. The notion of me is the first thought that comes in our mind before any other thoughts. Without the me, thinking is not possible. There is no need to deny the existence of me because it is part of thinking. Those who feel the need to deny the existence of me believe that thinking is our consciousness. Such writers are trapped in their minds without knowing it. By denying the existence of me, they affirm the existence of their own me. There must be someone to do the denying. In other words, you cannot deny the denier. Thinking is an acquired survival skill in consciousness. Thinking is useful in utilitarian matters. The me is part of it.

Why is there so much fuss made about the notion of me in spiritual books?

This indicates that some authors consider thinking as our consciousness and a valid source of spiritual information. They do not realize that thinking is an acquired skill and is essentially alien to our innate nonverbal consciousness. When our spiritual search is confined to the conceptual realm of thought, we favor some concepts and deny the value of other concepts in order to create a semblance of meaningful mental understanding. That is how the mental statement "There is no me" comes about. This is generally done without knowing that we are operating within the confines of closed conceptual loops. Conceptual spiritual knowledge gives us temporary intellectual appeasement because it belongs to the realm of our passing mental thoughts, which have no lasting effect on our permanent nonconceptual consciousness. Thoughts are not native to our nonverbal consciousness. We are born without thoughts.

Is conceptual spirituality misleading?

It helps those who rely on thoughts for spiritual knowledge. It can satisfy an intellectual need and give conceptual answers to conceptual questions. Conceptual spirituality may help beginners.

The common meaning of ego is the selfish activity of the mind. What does ego mean to you?

Ego is the entire thinking mind, not part of it. Our thinking depends on the ego. When our attention is absorbed by the activity of this ego-mind, it is oblivious to any other interest.

If the mind and ego are the same, does that mean every mental activity is selfish?

Not selfish in the pejorative sense. Mental activity is motivated by survival of the self.

What about selfless acts of heroism, acts of sacrificing one's own welfare for the sake of others, acts of generosity? These are acts of our thinking mind. Are they all motivated by survival of the self?

Yes. These selfless acts are also part of benefiting our own self. This is the way our ego-mind functions.

———

I know that spiritual truth is nonverbal and cannot be expressed with our conceptual language. But there must be something spiritually correct that can be said verbally. Is there?

What you call *spiritual truth* is the awareness of nonverbal consciousness you have at birth. But if you know that spiritual truth is nonverbal, why do you need to have a correct verbal description?

I miss the enjoyment I get from relying on verbal explanations. I feel uncomfortable when my mind is empty of ideas about spiritual truth. Ever since childhood, I always had very convincing answers to all my spiritual questions. I long for some form of mental satisfaction. Tell me, is there something my mind can rely on?

Verbally, the mind can say what spiritual truth is not.

I heard this and I know this. But we must be able to say what spiritual truth is. No?

No. Verbally it cannot be defined. It can be experienced nonverbally. Although, as you say, verbal spiritual knowledge gives you mental satisfaction, this type of satisfaction is temporary and can be lost. Why do you want more of something that you can lose? You also said you know that spiritual truth is nonverbal. But to know is not the same as to realize.

How do you realize?
You have to be in touch with your nonverbal consciousness. Once you become aware of nonverbal consciousness, it cannot be lost.

How is it done?
Your nonverbal consciousness is your attention. If you put your attention on your attention, you will instantly be in nonverbal consciousness.

———

What is self-knowledge?
The expression self-knowledge is an intellectual paradox. Strictly speaking, there is no self-knowledge in the way the mind knows, meaning conceptually. Out of the structural limitations of our language, we give the conceptual label of self-knowledge to the awareness of nonverbal self, which is understood to be our ever-present attention.

———

What is the mind, and what is the role of the mind in spirituality?
The mind is not our innate consciousness. It is part of the outside world in which it functions as a utilitarian tool. It is alien to the nonverbal consciousness we are at birth. And the role of the mind in spirituality is to demonstrate that we are not capable of experiencing or knowing our innate nonverbal consciousness through conceptual means.

Why is the mind part of the outside world and alien to the consciousness we have at birth? Isn't the mind our consciousness?

The mind is in our consciousness, but the mind is not our consciousness.

Can you explain what you mean?

Innate consciousness is the same for human beings no matter where they are born. Our minds develop while interacting with the outside environment, so we have different languages, cultural traditions, belief systems, and so on. Therefore, our minds are foreign to the permanent nonverbal consciousness with which we are born.

———

Does God write scriptures? I was told this in Sunday school, and it still bothers me today as an adult. I would like to know if scriptures are of divine origin. And are scriptures reliable at all?

Scriptures are written by people like you and me. Scriptures are verbal teachings that are limited to our mental understanding. They are primarily based on mythological beliefs created by our imagination. In general, scriptures have an allegorical value, not literal. Most of them lack the necessary scholarly rigor to be reliable historical records. Scriptures can be useful to satisfy the intellectual part of our mind.

But could they also have a negative influence? I would like to hear about that. As a child I had nightmares after hearing some biblical horror stories—for example, the so-called prediction of doomsday with salvation reserved for only the chosen believers. Today, as an adult, I witness with disbelief that these stories are taken seriously. There are also religious movements based on those doomsday beliefs. Is it necessary to have such scriptures?

Not all scriptures have such stories. Historians say that doomsday stories are mostly present in scriptures of the three Western religions of Judaism, Christianity, and Islam. They are an expression of our fragmented thinking trapped in an endless mental maze of fabricated mythological beliefs. As long as we are convinced thinking is consciousness and that thoughts describe spirituality correctly, we will have scriptures full of strange stories, including apocalyptic predictions. Confused thinking is the source of mythological beliefs. The inability to understand our consciousness creates mental apprehension and fearful thoughts, such as the end of the world as God's punishment. Then to escape our own terrifying thoughts, we seek mental comfort and solace in our own made-up figments of imagination, such as salvation for the chosen ones. We use fictitious beliefs to compensate for ignorance of who we are. When we no longer rely on thinking for spiritual knowledge, we no longer need to rely on scriptures. If we do not have this understanding, we remain prisoners of the literal interpretation of our scriptures. Such literal interpretations can be spiritually misleading and can have a negative influence.

Why don't we teach this starting at an early age?

The success of conceptual knowledge in utilitarian matters is overwhelming, so we do not realize that concepts cannot be used in matters of nonverbal undifferentiated consciousness. Through the I-inquiry we realize that our conceptual thoughts are an acquired cultural conditioning and alien to our innate consciousness. Once we understand, our children will be able to do the same by way of example. So we need to understand first.

———

What is the natural state?

We know this when we realize that thinking is not our innate consciousness.

How could that be? I am a student of philosophy. Without thinking, there is no philosophy.

The realization that thinking is not our innate consciousness occurs after a successful self-inquiry. Before that, we can try to explain this conceptually. Conceptual explanation does not replace the need for inquiry, but it can give us a verbal inkling into this question. So for example, hypothetically, if you were alone in the world, would you need to think?

I would need to think about how to defend myself from wild animals.

It is a theoretical question. Alone means no people, animals, or anything else, truly alone, nothing else. If you were totally alone, you would not need to think. Thinking is necessary to cope with this complex world. And because of this, we acquire the useful skill called thinking. Our innate consciousness is nonverbal, nondual, and without complexity. There is nothing to think about. You are born like that. This is the natural state.

———

What is karma?

It is a concept with many meanings, most often used loosely to imply destiny. Its original meaning is action or cause and effect.

What I really want to know is if there is karma or destiny?

This depends on your understanding of what thinking is. Does your thinking represent a reality independent of you, or is your thinking an idea in your mind?

I think of karma as independent of me.

So really your question is, does karma exist independently of my idea of karma?

Yes.

It is a typical dilemma we create for ourselves with our own mind because of incorrect or careless thinking. We do not make clear distinctions between abstract ideas and ideas that represent entities or objects in our world. You see, careless thinking wastes attention on unrealistic mental issues and confuses our understanding. We have logic to avoid confusion. If we are strict in our thinking, we cannot say that karma exists or that it does not exist independently of an idea in the mind. What we can say for sure is that karma exists as an idea in our mind.

But we have so many abstract ideas that have an independent existence. What about the idea of God? God is an abstract idea and has an independent existence. We believe that God exists outside of us.

Well, what you said is a perfect example of careless thinking. Here, too, we cannot say with certainty that God exists or that God does not exist independently from our mental idea of Him. But we can say that God exists as an idea in our mind.

———

Can what you say about karma be applied to our idea of reincarnation?

Yes.

———

Major world religions are based on mythological belief systems. Many of these faiths are named after teachers who

never intended to form religions. Long after they died, their teachings were politicized and mythologized to suit local sociopolitical needs and religious traditions. The little we know about their teachings from historical records clearly indicates the depth of their messages. However, the religions named after them are often the very opposite of the original message, full of silly dogmas, superstitions, mythological distortions of facts, and outright dangerous beliefs. Churches and temples are centers of ritualized theatrics to worship fictitious gods acquired from made-up scriptures. Is there any good that can come out of these religions?

Spiritual realization is nonverbal and therefore cannot be politicized or mythologized. Religions are a collection of mythological stories, easily understood and used as means to promote sociopolitical agendas that can have a positive influence on social behavior.

What about the atrocities that also come out of those religions?

Historians say that the atrocities are there too. An example is the extermination of one group of people by another because God made a particular land a promised land for one group but not for the other. This is a barbaric military conquest sanctioned by religion. Today such acts are called crimes against humanity and ethnic cleansing. There are many examples of these types of intellectual distortions and misconceptions in the holy scriptures, which are supposed to be words of God. Religions based on mental concepts are bound to give us fragmented understanding and distorted information. However, throughout recorded history there are individuals, whom we call enlightened ones, mystics, prophets, wise men, or Sons of God, who remind us that spirituality is nonverbal.

Was Christ enlightened like Buddha?
Not much is known about these individuals. They did not leave any written records. We know of them from writings done by others long after their departure. History is history. Intellectual spirituality can be learned from it. Your interest in it will have a limited effect on your nonverbal realization. After your mind is satisfied with historical knowledge, it can engage in the quest for nonverbal realization.

Yes. I am only venting my frustration about how I was misinformed by my religion as a child. I feel that it is criminal to raise our youth in historical falsehoods. We would be better off without such religions.
This is hypothetical. We cannot know that. Maybe your frustration will serve as a catalyst for realization.

——

Can absolute truth be known? If it can, what is it?
Absolute truth is an abstract concept fabricated by our mind. Apart from this mental notion, there is no such thing. Also, the notion of knowing is a mental concept. That which exists cannot be known mentally.

But that is only what the absolute truth is not. I am asking what absolute truth is.
As I said, absolute truth is a mental concoction. There is no such thing apart from an idea in the mind. You are chasing an intellectual mirage. Our mind can know what absolute truth is not. Nothing else.

I thought that you could provide the answer to this question.
Only if you discover the right way to ask this question.

What is the right way to ask?

First, find out who is asking. When you learn who the Questioner is, you will have the answer.

———

The other day I asked if absolute truth can be known. Now I have another related question. I understand that absolute truth is merely a concept fabricated by our fragmenting mind. But can scientific absolute truth be known?

In scientific matters, absolute truth is also an imaginary concept. Physical sciences have approximate truths that change with new understanding and are essentially interpretations of the perceived world. Scientific truths are not valid in all conditions in our vast universe. And yet in spite of it, conceptual, nonabsolute truths are reliable in utilitarian matters and useful for our physical survival on this planet.

I guess I should regretfully abandon my expectations that somewhere and someday I will come upon absolute truth.

To abandon your imaginary expectations is to realize that absolute knowledge is not possible with our conceptual minds. Our minds conceive many things and get caught in those manufactured beliefs. That is how our myths and religions are created. Get to know yourself first and become well acquainted with your own existence. The realization that the thinking mind can give us relative conceptual knowledge to be relied on in practical everyday life, not in matters of spiritual aspirations, is the fundamental nonverbal realization. From that moment on, our attention shifts from relying on verbal information available from our thinking mind to paying attention to our nonverbal consciousness, present in us from birth. This is how the mind becomes irrelevant in spiritual matters.

—

We know God by experiencing Him with our mind and thoughts, don't we?
Knowing is a mental function. So knowing God is the same as having an idea about God.

What is the difference between having an idea about God and experiencing God with our mind?
Both are concepts. Experiencing God is a mental idea of experiencing the idea of God in our mind.

I don't understand.
You assume there is an entity outside of you called God. Having assumed that, you created your own intellectual quandary and tried to solve it by asking these questions.

Do you mean that there is no God?
Not at all. I mean that there is God as an idea in your own mind, not an entity outside of you. So to experience or to know God is to experience or to know the idea of God in your own mind.

—

In a nutshell, what is required to become aware of our nonverbal consciousness? This will help me focus my attention on the most important aspect of it.
The most important part is the realization that our thinking mind is not our consciousness.

Is this the number one requirement?

Yes, it is by far the most important.

Can you explain why?

It is the opposite of what the vast majority of people are conditioned to believe. This conditioning is the most difficult obstacle to overcome. When we realize that we are nonverbal consciousness, our attention automatically makes an irreversible shift to our nonverbal consciousness with which we are born.

Why would that be so difficult? It seems that is such a simple thing to know.

Yes, but knowing about it mentally is not the same as realizing it. Look at yourself right now. You are asking intellectual questions because you think that thoughts are your consciousness.

——

I understand that thoughts are not capable of delivering nonverbal realization. But what role does thinking play in our inquiry? Thoughts must have some purpose, don't they?

Yes, they do. Thoughts play an important role in the inquiry process. We use thoughts to do the inquiry in order to dispel the erroneous belief that thoughts are our consciousness. The inquiry is a mental process done with our thinking mind. After we become aware of the presence of nonverbal consciousness, we realize that consciousness is not mental.

——

Is there a difference between spiritually realized people and people who follow common religions?

Can you be more specific with your question?

Is there a difference in their inner lives?

There is a big difference. People who follow religions are dependent on outside sources for their spiritual information. Their attention is outward-oriented. They are vulnerable to influence, control, or even manipulation by outside forces. Spiritually realized people have their attention turned inward. They know themselves and do not depend on external forces for their spiritual information. This is the most significant difference. It has a significant impact on personal life and social behavior. Now, are you aware that you asked me an abstract intellectual question and I gave you an abstract intellectual answer?

Yes, I know that my question is intellectual. I have no other way to relate to this subject. I know very little about nonverbal consciousness. I do have an inner urge to understand what spiritual life is like. That's why I asked this question.

Questions about your inner urge are best dealt with by looking for answers within yourself. Your question about other people is the result of being conditioned to look for answers outside instead of inside. We have been conditioned to believe that thinking is our main consciousness and to ignore the nonverbal consciousness with which we are born. Both have a purpose. Thinking is necessary for our practical phenomenal needs. Awareness of nonverbal consciousness is necessary for spiritual realization. In addition to your outward-oriented interests, use your inward-oriented ability.

What is inward-oriented ability?

It is our ability to inspect our own awareness.

How is it done?

You can do it by asking questions about where your consciousness comes from and who or what this consciousness is that you have had since birth.

This is what you mean by our inward-oriented ability.
Yes.

—

What changes in us when we realize that our true consciousness is nonverbal and divine and that we are born with it?
When we know that our consciousness is nonverbal and divine, we no longer expect spiritual knowledge from thinking. This shift of our attention is important to our spiritual understanding and daily life. Thinking is used for practical purposes, not for gaining spiritual knowledge. We can no longer be misled by conceptual or mythological beliefs.

—

I know that our thoughts are not meant to give us spiritual knowledge. I know how mental information is limited to matters in the phenomenal world. I have known this for many years, yet my mind wastes time thinking about the ultimate questions. My mind is trying to understand something I know it cannot understand. I am tired of it. Do you understand what I am saying?
Yes, I do. To know with your mind is not the same as realization.
How do I get to the stage of realization?
Realization occurs when the mental need to know is abandoned.
How can I abandon my need to know?
When you say you know that you know, this conviction blocks the awareness of nonverbal consciousness on which spiritual realization depends.

I heard your explanation about undifferentiated reality. You say existence is undifferentiated, but our utilitarian mind perceives it by dividing it into fragments called concepts or ideas. You also say conceptual statements have no spiritual value. But then isn't to say existence is undifferentiated a conceptual statement?

Yes, it is.

So how do we resolve this contradiction?

When we approach this matter on the verbal intellectual level, it is a contradiction. We do not rely on concepts for final spiritual knowledge. We use concepts to reach the nonverbal realization. Concepts are means, not goals. The goal is nonconceptual experience. Nonconceptual experience cannot be explained in any way other than language. Language contains fragmented perceptions called concepts. Concepts inherently contain contradictory meanings. Concepts are labels used like instruments for investigating our consciousness. The contradiction exists on the conceptual level.

Then how can I have a nonconceptual experience of undifferentiated reality?

Through the process of I-inquiry, our nonconceptual nonverbal self is revealed. Nonverbal experience of undifferentiated reality is essential.

The I-inquiry is too hard and too complicated. Is there anything simpler?

Try this. You experience your attention within you, don't you? You can feel or are aware of your attention. Yes?

Yes.

Your attention is the same as your *I* or the self. Ask yourself about who or what is this attention. When you become acquainted with the presence of your attention, you realize that your attention is the nonverbal consciousness with which you are born. This nonverbal consciousness is your experience of undifferentiated reality.

———

In psychology there are many methods to deal with depression. Depression is very common in modern, technologically advanced societies, but depression is virtually unknown in primitive societies.

In primitive societies, depression may be present and could be called sadness. Technologically advanced conditions may contribute to depression, but physical suffering can also cause depression. It is an academic subject for anthropologists and social psychologists. We can, however, talk about the reason for mental depression.

Yes. I agree. I am interested in understanding the reason for my depression.

As you said, there are many psychological methods to deal with depression. But there are also other ways, such as religious beliefs or faith in God, exorcism, shamanic rituals, and of course various drugs, medical and nonmedical. Awareness of nonverbal consciousness is not a therapy for depression; it is about understanding consciousness. In the process of learning about consciousness, understanding our thinking mind becomes essential. Faulty thinking is the cause of many human troubles, whether they be social, political, or personal.
What is faulty thinking?

When we identify with thinking as if it were our consciousness, that is faulty thinking. This faulty thinking is the result of cultural indoctrination, which convinced us that thinking and consciousness are the same. Until this error is revealed and understood, we are at the mercy of our thoughts and remain locked in the magical world of mental constructs. Either we are entertained with divine hope from spiritual beliefs, or we journey through the mental hell called depression. These experiences are part of our mental daydreams. Inquiry into the self addresses this faulty identification and demonstrates that our consciousness is nonverbal. Thinking is an acquired utilitarian skill, but it is not our consciousness. When this is understood, our thinking becomes a helpful tool that we use instead of being used by it.

—

How do you define brainwashing? I always understood it to be a derogatory term.

Yes, in common usage this term has a derogatory meaning. I am using it in a neutral sense, synonymous with the word *conditioning*. Conditioning is verbal and part of our thoughts. Most thoughts are imprinted in our mind during our cultural upbringing. In other words, we have been brainwashed since childhood without realizing it.

I received a very positive religious education. I don't call it brainwashing.

You can call it upbringing, training, or education. Nevertheless, it is your conditioning that happened to you due to the environment where you were born. When this conditioning is unacceptable to other social groups, they call it brainwashing.

I know. I also say that different religious groups received an unfortunate brainwashing when it is contrary to my beliefs.

Through the I-inquiry, we realize that mental conditioning is contrary to our nonverbal awareness and no different from indoctrination or brainwashing.

———

What happens when one realizes that thinking is not our consciousness?

That is the final realization and the end of our search. Our thinking is understood to be a tool for practical matters. We are free from the authority of thought. Our thinking mind is unimpaired in functioning as a utilitarian instrument. With this realization, we become spiritually mature and normal.

Why do you say normal?

Not to rely on conceptual beliefs for awareness of nonverbal consciousness is normal.

———

Is there anything that our thinking mind can know about nonverbal realization?

Yes. Our thinking mind can know that it cannot know.

———

I often focus my attention on my attention to relax my busy mind. I enjoy the feeling of boundless peace I get momentarily. I often wish that I could stay there longer. But my thoughts take over, and I become mentally active again.

I know what you mean by the nonverbal part of our consciousness. It is always there, waiting to be tapped. Is it normal that although I know how wonderful the feeling of nonverbal awareness is, I cannot stay there as long as I wish?
What you are doing is no different from meditation. It gives you temporary mental experiences that appear or disappear depending on the intensity of your mental concentration. When you focus intentionally on your attention, it is a form of meditation, which involves your mind. Therefore, you get a momentary experience or a mental feeling of, as you say, boundless peace. Even though this type of meditation is an effective means of relaxing your busy mind, it is a temporary concentration of the mind. This type of mental feeling is not the same as realization. Realization is a permanent condition due to direct knowing. It is not repeatedly focusing on your attention that is important, it is the realization that your attention itself is nonverbal consciousness and permanently present from birth. When we realize this once, this realization will stay in the background of our awareness. Although you may not focus on your attention intentionally, the realization that your consciousness is nonverbal will be permanently present in your awareness. It is not your thinking that is your consciousness. It is your nonverbal attention without mental sensations that is your consciousness.

———

I read that effort creates bondage. Don't we need effort to do the I-inquiry?
Effort is motivated by our ego, which leads to bondage. But since we are already in mental bondage, we can temporarily make

use of effort in our inquiry to extricate ourselves from mental bondage.

Wouldn't that create more bondage?

Yes, it can.

So what can we do?

You have to be aware that effort creates bondage.

That's all?

That's all.

——

I find it extremely difficult to live with a mind empty of spiritual thoughts. It is really impossible. My thoughts automatically try to grab on to what I believe I know, and soon after I find that what I know is nothing but ideas in my mind. So I return to the insecurity of the empty mind. Can this ever stop? I would like it to stop.

Why do you want it to stop? Wanting to stop is another idea in your mind.

Then what can I do?

When you realize that what you think you know about spirituality are words and any position your mind assumes is another thought, you will be still.

I feel uncomfortable, so I want to change it.

It is wanting to change that makes you uncomfortable, not the empty mind. A mind empty of spiritual misconceptions is comfortable. A happy and healthy mind is empty of spiritual beliefs.

——

This is the first time I have heard about nonverbal consciousness.

Where did it originate? Is it part of a religion?

It is mentioned in the Upanishads, which are philosophical writings from ancient India written a few thousand years ago. It is not a religion. It is based on reason, not on beliefs.

What do you teach?

The inquiry into the mind, which leads to awareness of our nonverbal consciousness.

Anything else?

Nothing else. Anything else would be dealing with beliefs.

———

I am intrigued by the emphasis on the *via negativa* approach to defining the ultimate spiritual realization. This approach seems to be quite prominent in Eastern traditions. Is there something similar in the West?

Are you referring to the Sanskrit word *neti neti*, meaning "not this, not this"?

Yes.

In Western philosophy, the word *indefinability* is used to convey the same meaning.

Why is it so important to use *neti neti* or indefinability to talk about the ultimate spiritual realization?

Positive verbal descriptions or definitions limit us to the mental level of understanding. If we rely on verbal spiritual information, we end up with words. Those words have a mesmerizing effect on our thoughts. Absorbed by words, we live and operate within the confines of our mind. So our attention is deflected away from our nonverbal consciousness. Spiritual awareness is nonverbal. Therefore, verbally we can say what it is not, not what it is. For the mind, spiritual realization is indefinable.

If spiritual realization is indefinable, how can we know it?
We cannot know it with our thoughts or our mind. We can realize it with our nonverbal self.

How can I know my nonverbal self?
By finding who you are. Ask yourself, what is this consciousness you refer to as *I*. You did not create this consciousness, did you?

No, I did not.
And yet you call it *I*. When you find this consciousness, you will know that your nonverbal self is not definable with words. Know yourself first.

———

A new realization plunged my mind into an alarming state of shock and disbelief. I just understood that all religions, philosophies, and spiritual disciplines with teachings based on thought-centered claims and beliefs are inherently inaccurate. They are not only incorrect but also deceitfully misleading. Is my realization correct, or am I in a state of irrational bewilderment and panic?
Your realization is correct. The bewilderment and panic is temporary. It is evidence of your disenchantment with the age-old cultural indoctrination that is imprinted on us from childhood, not for the sake of spiritual knowledge but for the sake of convenience.

What is the difference between scientific knowledge, spiritual knowledge, and religious knowledge?
Religious knowledge is based on fantasy, spiritual knowledge is based on awareness of our nonverbal consciousness, and scientific knowledge is based on mental abstract concepts.

All three are just concepts, aren't they?

Yes, they are. Our language is conceptual. So when we use it for communication, our expressions are conceptual.

If everything we know can only be expressed conceptually, can we know anything that is not conceptual?

Knowing is conceptual. Realization can be nonconceptual.

What is the difference between knowing and realization?

Knowing is a function of the mind. Realization occurs with awareness of our nonverbal consciousness.

We know what mental consciousness is. What is nonverbal consciousness?

We are born with nonverbal consciousness. The conceptual thinking mind is not our consciousness, it is an acquired skill developed through social conditioning.

So then religious knowledge, being a mental fantasy, and scientific knowledge, being abstract mental ideas, are both acquired mental skills. Spiritual knowledge, being based on awareness of our innate nonverbal consciousness, is nonverbal realization.

Yes.

———

What is the most common mistake we make as spiritual seekers?

Relying on our thoughts for spiritual knowledge.

You mean that we cannot rely on thoughts at all?

There is one aspect of thought that we can rely on.

Which aspect is that?

Thoughts can be relied on to tell us what spiritual truth is not.

———

I understand that you do not tell us in positive terms what non-verbal consciousness is because it would be only a verbal instruction, which limits us to mental knowledge. Is there anything that you can tell us verbally? In other words, is there a verbal teaching?

Verbally, I like to emphasize the importance of personal investigation into our consciousness. It is by investigating our consciousness that we can know who we are. Awareness of our nonverbal consciousness is spiritual realization.

———

I traveled to many countries visiting gurus. To my surprise and disappointment, I discovered that gurus often criticize, although in subtle ways, the teachings of other gurus. Why?

Until we realize that thinking is not our consciousness, we are restricted to the thinking mind in our understanding of spirituality. Mental spiritual knowledge is a form of intellectual ignorance. Mind-centered spirituality gives a fragmented point of view based on conceptual thinking that is different for every teacher, which leads to conflict and criticism. Those who engage in criticizing others still believe that spirituality based on our conceptual thinking mind can be valid, true, and absolute. When we realize that conceptual spirituality is misleading, criticism stops.

Spiritual truth is one and the same for everyone. Is it not?

This belief is your cultural conditioning. There is no such thing as one truth or truth for everyone. These types of statements are theoretical ideas in your mind, which limit you to the conceptual, fragmented way of thinking. There is no mental spiritual truth.

If there is no mental spiritual truth, is there truth at all?

The idea of spiritual truth itself is a concept in your mind. There is the realization that thinking is not our consciousness. After this realization, truth becomes an absurd mental idea.

I never heard this from any teacher.

Many spiritual teachings are based on a variety of mental ideas or mental fantasies fostered by different cultural environments. This is why the gurus you came across, as you yourself observed, disagree between themselves. The discord between religions is caused by the belief that there is an absolute spiritual truth based on our thoughts. There is no spiritual truth based on our thoughts.

Do we know spiritual truth when we realize that thinking is not our consciousness?

To know is a function of our thoughts. When we realize that thinking is not our consciousness, to know truth becomes irrelevant. What matters is the realization that we are nonverbal consciousness.

What is nonverbal consciousness?

It is the original and permanent consciousness we have at birth. Nonverbal consciousness is your divine nonverbal self. It is without thoughts.

I heard this concept many times before. This nonverbal self is the same in everyone. Is it not?

Yes, it is the same in everyone, but if you see it as a concept, it is then also an idea in your thoughts. By saying I heard this concept many times before, you express the belief that thinking is your consciousness.

———

Contemporary brain scientists tell us that sense perceptions give us incomplete and often distorted information about the world. At the same time we are told that theoretical scientists create universal laws, for example, $E = mc^2$. There seems to be a contradiction here. How do you understand the reliability of information generated by our mind and senses?

Mental and sensory perceptions are fragmented and partial knowledge.

Including universal laws?

Yes.

Can you explain why?

Universal laws are concepts created by our mental point of view. Mental information has a limited utilitarian application and is relevant to our survival needs. Concepts, including abstract theories, are implicitly partial mental understandings.

I don't follow why the notion of universal is a partial concept.

The concept of universal is partial because it is created by our fragmenting mind. We know nothing else about the universe except our limited ideas about it.

I agree with you, but within the scope and limitations of ideas, the scientific equations must be correct. Aren't they?

Yes, they are correct. But we also must remember that they are partial and limited because they come from our fragmented mental understanding. Scientific equations are the result of collective conceptual knowledge that develops through a long process of past intellectual achievements.

Is nonverbal knowledge not subject to change with new understanding?

Spiritual realization takes place within our nonverbal consciousness.

We are born with nonverbal consciousness that does not change. **I see. Scientists claim that the equation E = mc² answers the age-long question of where we come from. They say that we come from the Big Bang. What do you think?** Mental concepts are temporary explanations that change with new understanding. They are useful for our survival and can be pursued at the same time as we pursue spiritual knowledge about who we are as conscious beings. Those who claim to know where we come from do not realize that this question and the answer are pure mental conjectures of our fragmented imagination. This answer assumes that there is a beginning, which is another conjecture. If we follow this trend of thought, we will have to go from one assumption to the next without any end in sight. If we accept that we come from the Big Bang, the next question would be where does the Big Bang come from. This stops when we realize that our conceptual thoughts are not our consciousness but are an acquired survival skill in our consciousness. Conceptual equations can give us relative information about what exists in this world.

If this is so, it prompts another question about our convictions in the civil and religious areas. Are political doctrines and religious beliefs that are obviously conceptual and based on conjecture nothing more than a form of mental pollution? Some of it is, as you say, a form of mental pollution. But there are exceptions, such as the moral principle *love thy neighbor and love thy enemy*. Historians consider this principle as one of the highest pro-survival concepts regulating social life. Social and religious concepts of this type, although based on fragmented perceptions and conjecture, are useful for our survival.

I assume you think that knowledge of our nonverbal

consciousness is not a form of mental pollution. Can you say why?
Pollution is mental. We are born with nonverbal consciousness.

When you say that thinking is not our consciousness, I am afraid of losing the thinking ability I use for everyday activities and everything I know about the world and God. Is my fear normal and to be expected as part of spiritual progress?
The realization that thinking is not our consciousness does not stop your thinking. It gives you an additional perspective on where and when your thinking is necessary and where and when it is useless. For everyday activities it is necessary, but for knowing God it is ineffective. Your fear is caused by the way you rely on your thinking ability. You rely on thinking as if it were your consciousness.

Why is it so difficult to know our nonverbal self?
Our nonverbal self is always present. Mental effort absorbs our attention and prevents us from noticing it. Mental effort is usually motivated by our ego. So instead of seeing our nonverbal self, we exercise our ego.

Why are new converts so fanatical in their beliefs?
Fanaticism occurs within our thoughts. The belief that thinking is our consciousness engenders the belief that we are our thoughts

and thoughts are the source of absolute truth. Thus, the thinker and thinking are the same. These convictions fuse together and produce fanaticism. This is due to not knowing that thinking is a utilitarian tool.

What is the cure?

The cure is to realize that thinking is not our consciousness but is a tool for practical living.

Is this the most important nonverbal spiritual realization? I heard you say this so many times before.

Yes. It is the most important nonverbal realization. This spiritual realization frees you from the tyranny of your thoughts.

Is this called freedom from thought?

Yes.

———

I know that awareness of our nonverbal consciousness is not a religion. How would you define it? I would like to have a mental point of reference.

The nonverbal method of inquiry is based on logic and is like epistemology. A fairly accurate label for the awareness of our nonverbal consciousness would be pragmatic spirituality.

———

I understand and agree that religious beliefs based on concepts are often the cause of conflict between different faiths. I also know that religious communities provide useful social services. It seems that political and social doctrines are no different from religions. They are conceptual creations that often cause conflict between different societies and do good

works within their own groups. Routinely, ideological confrontations trigger violent reactions in one group and delight in the opposing group. There seems to be ideological confusion among us. I would love to know why.

Conceptual confusion is created by the faulty belief that thinking is our consciousness and that it represents absolute truth.

I have a hard time believing that every social or religious weakness is due to the faulty belief that thinking is our consciousness.

Relying on thinking as absolute truth is the main cause for our spiritual and social troubles. It is not enough to know this intellectually. This understanding is the result of personal realization. Do not expect that this realization is some exotic revelation coming down from the heavens with lightning and thunder. It is an ordinary realization that occurs when we investigate our consciousness. The realization that thinking is not our consciousness is so ordinary it can easily be overlooked, yet it is the most important and fundamental realization without which we will be endlessly roaming the infinite maze of thoughts.

——

I would like to discuss the concept that thinking is not our consciousness but is in our consciousness. It's not easy to grasp this idea. What would be the simplest way to understand it?

We are born without thoughts, but we are conscious. We are born with nonverbal consciousness, and as we grow we acquire thinking, which is stored in our consciousness. Although people are born with identical nonverbal consciousness, later they develop different languages and different ways of thinking. So obviously, thinking takes place in our consciousness, but thinking itself is not our consciousness.

I always thought that thinking makes us conscious.

This is the leading mental misconception we receive from cultural conditioning. The opposite is true. It is our innate nonverbal consciousness that makes thinking possible. Our nonverbal consciousness is permanent and stable. Thinking is changing and intermittent.

I can see the logic of your point of view, but still the overwhelming majority of people are convinced that thinking is our consciousness.

And that is precisely the reason the overwhelming majority of us follow religions based on thought-centered beliefs. Thought-centered beliefs are spiritual misconceptions.

Why?

Spiritual knowledge is nonverbal.

What is spiritual nonverbal knowledge?

Spiritual nonverbal knowledge is best understood as spiritual realization. This realization is not mental and does not take place in our thinking mind. It is a nonverbal experience occurring in our innate consciousness.

If this does not occur in our thinking mind, how do we know about it?

Not everything that we know is based on thoughts. We know that we exist without the participation of our thinking. It is a nonverbal experience. The nonverbal spiritual experience is called realization.

I never had a nonverbal spiritual experience called realization. How do we get this?

Through inquiry we realize that thinking is not our consciousness, but thinking occurs in our consciousness.

Why is it so important to realize that thinking is not our consciousness?

Without this realization, we remain trapped in our mental web.

So you say it is through inquiry that we come out of this mental web. What kind of inquiry is it?

It is our ability to inspect our consciousness. For example, inquire who or what is this innate nonverbal consciousness you experience and refer to as *I*. When you find who or what it is, you will navigate with ease through the maze of this mental web.

―――

Religious conditioning is powerful and convincing. I become emotional when I hear dramatic religious stories. Although I know that they are just words, they have a powerful influence on my psyche. I feel elated and spiritual. I sometimes wish that this feeling would last longer, but it fades away as quickly as it came. Is there any spiritual value in emotional religious experiences?

These experiences may be an indication that we are open and ready for lasting nonverbal spiritual realization. Spiritual realization is the result of understanding our innate nonverbal consciousness. This understanding is different from mental or verbal religious conditioning. It is a realization that our innate nonverbal consciousness is the divine nonverbal self. This realization gives us a lasting sense of spiritual peace and harmony, whereas religious beliefs are short-lived and fluctuate with changing emotions. As you indicated, such feelings can appear and disappear on their own. If we are capable of religious emotional feelings, the same feelings can easily turn into excessive religious fervor or even fanatical behavior. Religious conditioning may sometimes be helpful in our spiritual quest. However, it can also be unreliable and sometimes even dangerous.

I have been meditating for over forty years. I still do, but not in a formal way. Meditation is now part of my life. When I listen to you, to my surprise, you say what I have learned through meditation. Spiritual realization is not anything extraordinary or supernatural. It is the ordinary awareness of our nonverbal consciousness. This simple awareness is the answer to our spiritual aspirations.
I agree.

If meditation produces the same realization, how do we know which path to follow?
The one you are attracted to. The method of inquiry is based on reason, not on spiritual practice.
It's not known what path is better or best?
No, it's not. There are many ways.

You insist that every spiritual claim must be verified by experience. Are there other spiritual disciplines with a similar requirement?
Most mystics emphasize, in one way or another, the importance of experience instead of mental belief. Often it is expressed in symbolic or poetic ways, but it can also be expressed in plain

language. Early Christians known as Gnostics used the term *gnosis*, which refers to the insight or nonverbal experience that is necessary for understanding one's relationship with the divine.

———

It's frustrating to see the world so confused. No individual, no political group, no country, nobody knows what the right way to live is. Instead of peace and harmony, we have war and discord. The world is falling apart, continuously. Nobody cares. Is there an end to this?

According to you, what is the best way for the world to live?

I don't know. I thought people in this meeting, wise people who meditated for forty years, would know. All I know is the world is a mess, and I want to help make it better.

To understand the world, you need to understand yourself. To understand yourself, you need to find out who or what is the consciousness you call *I*. Find out who says *I*. You need to know who this *I* is who wants to change the world. This realization will make you a better helper.

———

After meditating for many years, I am now interested in awareness of nonverbal consciousness. I am frustrated when some of your statements challenge my mental conditioning and get me entangled in too much thinking. Then I go back to my meditation to quiet my mind, and it works. My mind becomes quiet.

If you get entangled in too much thinking, meditation will quiet your mind. When you realize that thinking is not your consciousness but is an acquired tool for dealing with practical matters, thinking will no longer entangle you.

—

What is the best way to learn how to discern between dangerous and useful beliefs? I think that society at large has not learned this yet.

This becomes possible when we recognize that beliefs are part of our utilitarian thoughts but not absolute spiritual truths.

Don't we need to cultivate useful positive beliefs?

Positive practical beliefs are needed to improve our conditions for survival. But we also need to be aware that having positive beliefs does not keep us safe from dangerous beliefs. They are thoughts, and thoughts are intrinsically unstable. When circumstances change, they can become negative or dangerous beliefs.

Then what is the remedy?

The remedy is the realization that thinking is not our consciousness. Beliefs are mental concepts that keep us trapped in the mind. Spiritual realization is not a concept. It is awareness of our existing nonverbal consciousness we have at birth. Awareness of nonverbal divine consciousness is void of good, bad, or neutral beliefs.

—

What is moksha? I read stories of world religions where this word is often mentioned. What is the English translation?

This is a Sanskrit term used in Hinduism. The literal translation of moksha is "liberation." It can also mean nonverbal realization. Also, in popular mythological stories it means being free from karma.

What is liberation?

We have been raised to believe that thinking is our consciousness. When we realize that thoughts are not our consciousness, we become liberated from the thought-dominated mind. This condition is called moksha or liberation.

How can this also mean being free from karma?

Hindus believe that our cultural conditioning is our karma.

——

I understand that the strength of our thinking is unbelievably powerful, and it is also like a double-edged sword. On the one hand, our thinking leads us to commit heinous atrocities, and on the other hand, our thinking creates acts of compassion and selfless bravery. Our thinking controls our daily activities. Are we slaves to our thinking?

Yes, we are slaves to our thoughts until we realize that we are not our thinking and thoughts are not our consciousness.

Why don't we realize this?

Due to cultural indoctrination, we believe that our thinking mind gives us reliable truth. Our civilization is still in the dark ages as far as knowledge of the architecture of human consciousness goes. Ten thousand years of recorded history shows little progress in this area. The main obstacles are religious and political dogmas. Mental conditioning is powerful because it is imprinted on us at an early age. Those who indoctrinate us do not know what they are doing because they themselves have been indoctrinated by the generations before them. We call this our cultural tradition, of which we are proud. But we need to be conscious that along with positive social teachings we also get a tradition of prejudice. This process has gone on for thousands of years and continues today.

This seems to be a hopeless situation.

Not totally. We also know that during the entire period of recorded history we have had spiritual leaders who tried to free us from the tyranny of dogmatic beliefs. But talking about history with intellectual generalities, as we are doing now, will not produce spiritual realization. What really matters is the realization that thoughts by themselves have no power. Thoughts are acquired mental instruments developed for our survival needs. We are in control of our thoughts when we become aware of who we really are. This awareness is possible when we investigate our innate consciousness. We need to know who or what is this consciousness that we refer to as *I*. When we realize that we are not our thoughts, thoughts are not our consciousness, and each one of us is born with a divine nonverbal consciousness called the nonverbal self, then any authority, religious or secular, can no longer indoctrinate us. We can no longer be enslaved by our thoughts. We are free from the oppressive power of thought.

———

I have been studying spirituality for many years. Freedom from thoughts has been my number one goal from the beginning. I follow and understand much of what you say about nonverbal consciousness. I know the value of the I-inquiry to realize our nonverbal self. I know how limited verbal understanding of spirituality can be and the importance of our awareness of nonverbal consciousness. I also know

that thinking is not my consciousness. I occasionally have glimpses of freedom from thoughts as a result of my deep insight into the meaning of *who am I* during inquiry. I also experience freedom from thoughts during my concentration on a mantra in meditation. Yet all these experiences are short-lived. I have never experienced lasting freedom from thoughts. My mind sneaks up on me again and again, and I find myself unable to stop thinking. What is the reason for this continuous thinking?

You know that the *I* is the first thought in our mind and the common denominator of other thoughts. Thinking is not possible without the presence of our *I*.

Yes, I read that, and I know this.

Well, since your thinking is dependent on your *I*, you need to realize what is the makeup of your *I*. If your *I* is the verbal definition of who you believe you are, other thoughts can exist because you hold on to the thoughts about who you are. It is not by dealing with those thoughts through concentration on a mantra or other method that you can be free from them. It is by abandoning thoughts about yourself that those other thoughts will not arise. How do we abandon thoughts about ourselves? Well, we need to be aware that ideas about ourselves are words accumulated during our lifetime. The mind is in a habit of, as you said, sneaking up on us again and again. If you pay attention, you will notice that those thoughts always start with thoughts about yourself. And if even one thought about yourself is present, whether it be good, bad, or neutral, you cannot be free from other thoughts. This realization is necessary to have a lasting experience of freedom from thoughts.

———

What is the meaning of freedom from thoughts? Does it mean no thoughts at all, or does it simply mean being free from unwanted thoughts that can control us?

It means being free from unwanted thoughts that can control us. Useful thoughts are tools that are wanted and necessary. They do not control us. There is no need to be free from useful tools. We are in control of them. We need to be free from useless thoughts, the accumulated cultural misinformation. We need to be free from the misplaced power we have invested in erroneous thoughts. The meaning of freedom from thoughts is the realization that thoughts are practical instruments and not a source of absolute spiritual knowledge.

———

Can you elaborate on cultural misinformation from which we need to be free?

Apart from misinformation in the form of religious indoctrination and the cultural convention that we are part of a specific social group with a specific social status, the most pertinent misinformation is the conditioned belief that we are individuals with a unique role to play and are encouraged to represent and defend. These definitions about what we are supposed to be engender specifically predetermined interpretations of the world around us. Culturally programmed beliefs attached to the *I* are verbal fabrications that have little in common with the nonverbal consciousness we have since birth. This is what is meant by cultural misinformation from which we need to be free.

———

Ever since I realized that thinking itself does not give me any important information about spirituality, my thinking mind no longer assumes a dominant role. Most of the time it remains clear and alert, watching the world as if it were a play with tragedy and joy in which I can and I should, at any moment, participate if need be. I feel comfortable with my new awareness. I do not have a question, but I felt the urge to share these thoughts.

Thank you for sharing your thoughts.

———

Conventional education promotes the development of the mind. Your emphasis seems to be on nonverbal consciousness. Don't animals have nonverbal consciousness? Why do humans need nonverbal consciousness?

Animal consciousness may be similar to the nonverbal consciousness we have at birth. As adults we ignore our innocent nonverbal state. A means to restore awareness of our nonverbal consciousness is called I-inquiry. It requires a strong, developed, logical mind to successfully conduct inquiry into what essentially is the mind itself.

———

I read that mental or verbal knowledge is indirect knowledge. I would like to understand what direct knowledge is.

Knowledge obtained through our senses and mind is indirect knowledge. Direct knowledge is awareness of one's own existence. This nonverbal knowledge of one's own existence is also the direct knowledge of our nonverbal self.

I thought that the realization of our nonverbal self is more elaborate and difficult, not simply knowledge of our existence or that I am.

This seemingly insignificant direct nonverbal realization cannot be anything else but our nonverbal self.

———

I have a nagging question that bothers me. How do I become free from thought?

By realizing that thoughts are not you.

How do I realize that?

By knowing who you are.

How do I know who I am?

By realizing what this consciousness is that you call *I*.

———

"Not to know is to know": what does that mean?

This statement refers to the nonverbal realization that innate nonverbal consciousness cannot be known with our thinking mind.

———

I love my dog. When I look into her eyes, I see God consciousness. Is our nonverbal consciousness the same as animal nonverbal consciousness?

The essence of nonverbal consciousness is the same in us and in life as well as in the principles regulating visible and invisible substances. Existence is consciousness.

**Why do numerous spiritual disciplines emphasize the impor-
tance of the *I am*?**

The notion of *I am* is often used as a synonym for ultimate spiritual
realization because we realize our own existence without the
help of our thinking mind. It is a way to be in touch with our
nonverbal consciousness.

Do you use the *I am* notion to explain nonverbal consciousness?

Yes, I do. In the West the *I am* is shrouded in mysterious meanings
and has many strange connotations. It is mentioned in the Bible
and many esoteric theories have been proposed about it, which
adds to our verbal confusion. I prefer to use the notion of attention, which is also nonverbal and easily experienced. Our attention is the same as the *I am*, the nonverbal self, and our innate
nonverbal consciousness.

**If our attention, which is so easy to experience, is the same as
our nonverbal self, why is so much fuss made about realizing
the nonverbal self?**

There is no need for any fuss. Our attention is our nonverbal self.

Is it really that simple?

Yes.

**I know there are many ways to be happy. I want so much to be
spiritually fulfilled. What is happiness?**

See if this makes sense. Happiness is the joy the mind experiences
when it knows it is free from the need to know.

The essence of religion is belief in the unbelievable. Why are we so naïve?

Most of us are convinced that unbelievable and supernatural beliefs are part of reliable knowledge. We are unaware that these beliefs are archaic ideas acquired from cultural indoctrination.

Why is belief in the supernatural so common?

Believing in the supernatural is a common superficial spirituality. It is an archaic superstition well established in our culture. The notion of the supernatural is an idea made up in our imagination. Thinking is a useful tool to deal with survival matters, not with figments of imagination.

What can we do to change this?

Learn about consciousness.

—

You say that knowledge depends on imagination and assumption. It is indirect mental information defined by concepts. You also say that direct knowledge, without assumption, is our own consciousness. Why is this not an assumption?

You are consciousness. Are you asking if you are an assumption?

I see the logic of what you are saying. It makes sense. But when you say you are consciousness, is this statement an assumption?

Verbal statements are assumptions.

I agree. So this statement is indirect knowledge, yes?

Yes, it is.

So how can I have direct knowledge?

When your attention abandons verbal statements and acknowledges the actual presence of your innate consciousness, you have direct knowledge.

———

I heard you say we need to ask the *who am I* question to understand our consciousness. You also say the mind cannot know the answer to this question because the consciousness we are born with is nonverbal. If this is so, why ask the question? It's a contradiction.

When you ask *who am I* you discover that your thinking mind is incapable of knowing the answer. This discovery leads you to the realization that I am nonverbal consciousness. The *who am I* question is an intellectual stratagem for understanding consciousness.

———

More than thirty years after my divorce, I still feel anger and discomfort whenever I think about it. Psychotherapy, meditation, friends, and the passage of time helped, but none of these erased the pain and the memory of it. Can the knowledge of nonverbal consciousness be useful to deal with unhappiness caused by marital conflict that occurred a long time ago?

The memory of the event indicates that you have a sound mind. Memory cannot and should not be removed. Memory is there to be used.

How can painful memories be used?

Since the pain persists, there is a need for more understanding.

I am tired of more and more understanding. I am a graduate of psychology and quite savvy about the complexity of the human psyche. I sought outside help without hesitation and tried various self-improvement programs. The pain still

lingers. I want to be done with it for good.

The way you asked the question and your belief about being savvy regarding the complexity of our psyche indicates that you expect to solve your inner pain through mental knowledge.

How else can I tackle this? I am raised and educated to do it this way. If there is another way, I want to know, and that is part of my question.

You are tired of mental or conceptual understanding, which did not produce the desired results. Mental understanding is limited to your thoughts. As you said, our psyche is complex, so maybe you need to tackle this issue from a nonconceptual angle. You asked if knowledge of nonverbal consciousness is a concept you can use. This is a typical intellectual approach that comes directly from your thinking mind. Nonverbal consciousness is not a concept. Nonverbal consciousness is a label given to a state of awareness within us that is not made of thoughts.

How is this possible? Our awareness and thoughts are the same.

You are born without thoughts. But you are born with consciousness. You acquire thoughts later from your environment. Thoughts are not part of your original consciousness.

My original consciousness has no meaning. It is empty.

It is empty of verbal meaning, but it is full of your own consciousness.

How can empty consciousness be of any use?

Acknowledging our empty consciousness indicates that in addition to our thoughts, we have this nonverbal consciousness about which you were asking.

How can knowing about our nonverbal consciousness be useful?

Knowing about it mentally makes little difference. Realizing it makes a big difference.

How does one realize it?

All right, that is a good question. So listen. I will explain how you can realize nonverbal consciousness using the nonverbal method called the I-inquiry. Do you know anything about non-verbal consciousness?

Almost nothing. I only heard about it from a friend who suggested I attend your talk.

This method was originally outlined in the Upanishads, which are philosophical writings conceived in India thousands of years ago. This inquiry method is still a living tradition today. There are no beliefs to follow, and it is not a religion. It is a discipline of investigation into our consciousness and is based on reason. The I-inquiry is the *who am I* question. So when you ask this question, the first ideas that come to mind are notions about ourselves we accumulated during our lifetime. But that is our verbal information about who we are. If we continue questioning, we inevitably realize that we really do not know who we are, and our mind experiences a sort of blankness or void. Most of us abandon the question at this point. But if we stay with the inquiry, we come to the realization that no one else but ourselves perceives this mental void. I am the perceiver of my own void. Now, listen carefully. Do not discount this seemingly ordinary realization. The perception of this mental void is the realization of nonverbal consciousness. It is easily overlooked.

It is very subtle. But I still do not see what significance it can have in my life.

You can understand this intellectually at first. After that, when we continue the *who am I* inquiry, we can ask what is this consciousness that perceives my mental void. When we persist in questioning, we realize there is a presence within us, which we can label attention. The awareness of our attention is a practical way of perceiving the presence of our nonverbal consciousness since the attention itself is nonverbal too. The significance of this realization is we now know we are nonverbal consciousness in addition to the verbal description of who we are.

I understand it intellectually, but I do not have the experience of nonverbal consciousness.

Maybe you are expecting to have a verbal experience given to you by your thoughts. The nonverbal consciousness is what the word nonverbal implies. It is nonverbal. You can know it as a presence, not as a thought.

Is nonverbal consciousness the same as the concept of soul?

The word *soul* can be used as a label to describe it. But look at what you are doing. You want to have a word to hang on to instead of seeing this soul as the presence of your nonverbal consciousness. Nonverbal consciousness is a permanent presence. It is present when you say I am. It is present when you say I don't know. It is present when you put your attention on your attention. It is present when you are awake or asleep. It is always present. It is your consciousness with which you are born, and it will always be with you. And this nonverbal consciousness is you. You are not your thoughts. This is the realization that you get from the I-inquiry.

How does this relate to the traumatic memory of my divorce thirty years ago?

During the process of learning about the richness of our consciousness, inquiry demonstrates that thoughts assume the role of our entire awareness without leaving any role for our nonverbal consciousness. Survival requires our mind to dominate everything we know about who we are and what our task and purpose is in the world. We created elaborate systems of verbal convictions and beliefs, called religion, culture, and civilization, that confine us to the intellectual mental realm. We became oblivious to the nonverbal, unconditioned, and unbound core of our

consciousness. Lacking awareness of our nonverbal consciousness, we believe thinking is our consciousness. Like most of us,
you, too, are a victim of this agelong cultural conditioning.
Maybe the word *victim* is too strong.
Maybe not. We are victims of indoctrination. So listen carefully. As
long as you believe thinking is your consciousness, you believe
thoughts define you. When you remember your divorce, you
think that those memories are you. The memories of your divorce are thoughts occurring in your consciousness. That is why
it is important to know *who am I*. The I-inquiry demonstrates
that you are not what your thoughts tell you. You are nonverbal
consciousness. Of course, it is not enough to know this intellectually, but you can realize this when you do the I-inquiry.
After this realization, your attention shifts by itself to your nonverbal consciousness, and thinking becomes a useful tool for
survival. Your attention resides in the nonverbal consciousness
with which you are born. When thinking is understood not to
be your consciousness, the memories of past events are seen as
memories, nothing else. Eventually there will be a time when
you will be laughing at how absurd it was that you believed your
thinking was you.

———

**I have a hard time accepting that relying on verbal knowledge
in spirituality is misleading. Religions are based on verbal
information, and the vast majority of people follow these
religions.**
Throughout history new thinkers, new philosophers, new religious
leaders, new gurus, and prophets appear and attract large fol-
lowings. Does this mean that many of us instinctively feel

dissatisfied with the prevalent verbal teachings of our religions? Even you, did you not come here to seek something more than what you get from your cultural conditioning?

Oh, I see.

I gave you an intellectual answer to your intellectual question. It may or may not be correct. What is more important is to first know who is questioning. To know what verbal conditioning is, you need to know who or what the consciousness is to which you refer as *I*.

———

I heard you say that Existence, with a capital *E*—meaning everything that exists, including us—is an undifferentiated reality. Am I right? Did I understand you correctly?

Yes, you did.

Then why is it that we do not see it this way? What we see is a multitude of objects and creatures. This intrigues me. I want to know how I can see this world in the non-differentiated way.

The way you ask this question indicates you want to understand non-differentiated reality mentally. Our mental ability to understand is based on differentiating or fragmenting our perceived reality. It is a dilemma. Any question asked with our mind gives us a fragmented, conceptual, differentiated answer. Non-differentiated reality is the label given to a nonverbal realization that occurs as a result of knowing who or what our *I* is. Therefore, in order to realize what non-differentiated reality is, we need to first understand who is asking the question. If you rely on your thinking mind that says you are so-and-so and separate from the rest of the world, then you see the multitude of things, and you are also part of that differentiated plurality. But when you realize you are nonverbal consciousness, you can then see the world in an undifferentiated way.

Do you see the world in an undifferentiated way with your eyes? Not with your eyes. The word *see* refers to the eye of nonverbal consciousness. The poetic expression for this is the "eye of the soul."

So the realization of who I am or what is my *I* is the answer. Yes. The *I* is the common denominator of our thoughts. What I think I am determines the substance of what I think about. So the realization of *who am I* is the answer to questions about nonverbal consciousness, including non-differentiated reality.

———

What is zero-thought-consciousness? How do I experience it? How do I know about it? When I try to know it, I do it with my thoughts, don't I? And why is it important to know about zero-thought-consciousness?
Zero-thought-consciousness is a label for nonverbal consciousness. Out of habit you think you can verbally know nonverbal consciousness. When you say that you want to experience it, do not expect to have a verbal experience, like another thought. Thoughts start and end, and you can experience them. But nonverbal consciousness is realized by noticing it. It is always there. We are born with it. Notice that your attention is without thoughts, and this is the nonverbal consciousness. The awareness of our ever-present attention is this zero-thought-consciousness. When we know we are born with this nonverbal consciousness, we realize that we cannot expect any significant spiritual information from our acquired thinking mind. The knowledge that we are this innate nonverbal consciousness is

the answer to our spiritual aspirations. That is the importance of being aware of zero-thought-consciousness.

———

You say that our thinking ability cannot be relied on in spiritual matters. Can thinking be relied on 100 percent in scientific or utilitarian matters and in many other practical life endeavors?

It can be relied on, but not 100 percent. Scientific laws are based on abstract values and can be relied on in theoretical calculations. But for practical purposes, 100 percent reliance is not possible and not necessary. As long as it works and gives acceptable results, it is good enough.

If scientific laws are not 100 percent reliable in practical applications, how can our thinking ability give us absolute truth in any life endeavor?

The idea of wanting to rely on our verbal ability for absolute truth in any endeavor indicates we do not understand that our life depends on our innate nonverbal consciousness. Absolute verbal truth based on thinking is not absolutely required in our life.

It is disappointing, and I feel insecure to hear you say this. Relying on my thinking and believing that truth can be known gives me peace of mind. Although I don't know what that truth is, I hope to find it with my own thinking mind.

Truth based on thinking is mere words. Our belief that truth can be known verbally is our cultural conditioning. Our thinking can be helpful, but it can also be dangerous. It is helpful when used as a tool for practical endeavors. It is dangerous when it is vested with absolute truth, like in sociopolitical doctrines and religious dogmas. Doctrines and dogmas are verbal fantasies.

History is full of examples. Mental peace of mind based on fragmented thoughts is short-lived. Peace of mind occurs when the thinking mind no longer seeks to know truth, and this happens when you realize that you are not your thinking mind. Nonverbal consciousness does not give any verbal or conceptual truth to follow. Instead, first know who the thinker is who wants to know absolute truth.

———

I am a student of science. I heard you say that what is usually understood as the objective world is really subjective. If so, our scientific laws would then be nothing more than subjective opinions.

Scientific laws are interpretations of subjective perceptions occurring in our mental awareness. These laws exist in our thinking mind, not outside of it. We do not discover laws in the outside universe. We formulate new mental interpretations based on our subjective perceptions of the world. Our thinking mind gives us manufactured ideas about a world that exists in our mind. So we realize that this knowledge is subjective. In other words, it means that what we know about the world is subjective. Civilization depends on our subjective mental perceptions, not on the so-called objective worldview. Our subjective understanding propels our civilization.

I have a hard time accepting this. So the scientific point of view that the world is objective and independent of our perceptions is wrong?

As a scientist you know that science is based on abstract assumptions. The objective existence of the world is a working assumption necessary to formulate scientific laws.

This is hard to accept. How can the world be an assumption?
The notion of existence and the notion of the world are verbal concepts. Concepts about the world are concepts. They are not the world. They are concepts.

I think that concepts about the world are not different from the world.
I will give you an example of how science relies on assumptions. Take the notion of time. In order to have time you need to assume that there is a beginning. So some scientists think that the Big Bang was the beginning of our universe. From the latest scientific calculations, the universe is supposed to be 13.7 billion years old. Other scientists do not think that there is a beginning, and if there was a Big Bang, it was one of many explosions that occur cyclically and continuously. For them the universe is eternal, timeless. So do we know for sure that there is or is not a beginning? As you can see, most of these statements are abstract scientific assumptions, and they are subjective.

———

I came across the concept of synchronicity in a book of spiritual teachings. I like this concept. Do you teach about synchronicity?
No, I do not. Mental concepts are meant to appease the restlessness of the mind by creating an appearance that the mind can understand the problems it created in the first place. Many spiritual or religious teachings fulfill this mental need efficiently and convincingly. If you believe in concepts, you are locking yourself in the confines of an unending mental maze of ideas.

———

What is the meaning of *Sat-Chit-Ananda*?

It is a Sanskrit label for our nonverbal divine consciousness we have at birth.

How do you translate it?

Sat means "existence." *Chit* means "intelligent consciousness." *Ananda* means "beatitude" or "bliss" and also "happiness."

Can this nonverbal divine consciousness be called the soul?

It can, but it is understood as the nonpersonal soul, more like God consciousness.

———

You do not believe in illusion, yet I read in the Upanishads that the world is an illusion. I am confused.

Most probably the Upanishads you read belong to the Vedanta tradition, which is a form of Hindu religious dogma. Through inquiry we learn that the way we perceive the world as separate from us and God is an illusion. The world itself is not an illusion.

———

What is the meaning of "that which is is not knowable"?

Existence, with a capital *E*, cannot be known with our thinking mind. Why? Our thinking mind gives us subjective mental interpretations of what exists. Our mind operates with concepts, and concepts are fragmented perceptions of what is.

———

Prayer and meditation have been used by religions for thousands

of years with positive results. How does the method of I-inquiry compare?

Prayer and meditation are mental concentration on a divinity or mantra fashioned by our mind. They require continuous practice. This practice keeps our spiritual awareness within the confines of our thoughts. I-inquiry reveals the existing divine consciousness that we are at birth. It needs to be realized once. In this type of inquiry, our spiritual awareness is liberated from the confines of our thinking mind. This I-inquiry has also been known for thousands of years.

———

There are many minor religions and five major world religions with hundreds of different denominations claiming their unique brand of spiritual teachings as being the best and true. But with awareness of our nonverbal consciousness, we realize that these claims are based on the erroneous belief that thinking is our consciousness. Verbal information is intrinsically flawed because it is fashioned by our fragmenting thinking mind. This mind is an acquired instrument of survival, not a source of spiritual information. If this is so, then one cannot rely on our collective spiritual information. This realization creates a void in my consciousness, which makes me run back to the comfort of my familiar religious beliefs. Is it possible to live without beliefs and not feel lost?

If you conduct a thorough inquiry into the makeup of our thinking mind, you will know not to consider conceptual information as reliable spiritual knowledge. The discomfort with conceptual void is due to your unquestioned habit of relying on your thinking mind. To experience this insecurity is an indication that you have performed some initial and useful inquiry into the makeup of your mind. Further inquiry will remind you that you are born without your conceptual mind but with consciousness void of any beliefs or convictions. You are born without thoughts. Once you realize this, you will no longer be afraid of mental void. This does not mean that you will always be without thoughts. So listen carefully. As you already know, our thinking mind is an acquired survival tool. Practical thoughts pertaining to our physical survival are needed. They are essential and need to be continuously improved. Scientific information is part of those utilitarian useful thoughts. Philosophical, psychological, and sociopolitical information can be helpful in communicating our desires for better survival conditions. Spiritual information is the result of our ability to create mythological fantasies and needs to be understood as such. Our power of imagination is useful for practical needs, not for spiritual knowledge. A clear distinction needs to be acknowledged between our thinking and our innate nonverbal consciousness. Unless we realize that this difference exists, we will be running back to our familiar mental beliefs whenever we face our nonverbal consciousness. And yet it is in this nonverbal consciousness, void of any beliefs and convictions, that we find our spiritual security.

I clearly follow what you are saying. But I understand it only intellectually. How can I establish myself in this realization without feeling lost?

To realize this, you need to know what is the core of your being. This can be established with self-introspection called the I-inquiry. So again, listen carefully. When you ask yourself *who am I*, your mind will have to say I don't know because the mind actually does not know, and it cannot know. Then when you ask who knows that the mind does not know, you will have to admit it is your own consciousness that knows this. This consciousness is you. You are this innate nonverbal consciousness void of any conceptual thoughts. When you realize this even once, you will never again run to your pet beliefs, religious or secular.

——

Scientists successfully located the Higgs boson particle. This particle is elementary, stable, and present everywhere. Therefore, it is called the God particle. But scientists say that it is not what they expected because boson is unstable and appears to be temporary. This raises more new questions instead of giving the final answer about the original building blocks for the creation of this world. Scientists continue the research with new and improved equipment. Is our scientific research doomed to continue without ever finding the answer to the origins of the world?

The goal of science is to understand the physical world but not necessarily to answer made-up theoretical questions based on beliefs.

Science does not follow beliefs.

The idea that the world has a beginning is a belief. Scientists try to avoid unverifiable beliefs but cannot always succeed in bypassing cultural collective conditioning.

You mean that science and religion share the common belief that there is a beginning of the world?

Yes.

Is there no beginning to our world?

Beginning is a mental idea. It is an assumption derived from another belief that the universe is expanding. But this assumption does not explain why there is expansion or how the space to expand is created. As long as we rely on the naïve assumption that there is a beginning to our world, we will end up with a naïve conclusion. These are assumptions upon assumptions, no different from beliefs found in religions.

If this is true, it is a disturbing thought. Is our understanding of the world so uncertain and useless?

Uncertain, yes, but not useless. Our understanding of the world is conceptual. Concepts are intrinsically unstable and therefore what we can see with our thinking mind is unstable too. It is, however, useful enough to apply this virtual and relative knowledge to improve our chances of survival in this unstable universe of ours. As you said, we are "doomed," or as I would say, we are urged by our own innate life force to continuously learn about the conditions of our existence in this phenomenal, unstable, always changing world. Our conceptual scientific mind is well suited as an instrument of survival, but when the same mind ventures to explain fabricated abstract ideas, such as our origin or who created the world, it does this as an entertaining mythology.

———

You say that there is no verbal spiritual realization. It implies that there must be some other form of realization. That other form you call the nonverbal spiritual realization. I have no idea what it means. Is there some other way to say what you mean?

Obviously one cannot say or explain verbally what nonverbal means.

I mean, what is nonverbal spiritual realization?

It can be experienced, not explained.

How do you experience it?
For example, when you realize that verbal meanings do not and cannot give you spiritual realization, this understanding itself is the experience of nonverbal spiritual realization.

———

Why is there such a huge discrepancy between conventional spirituality and what you are saying about being aware of nonverbal consciousness?
The conventional approach is based on the belief that our thinking can give us spiritual knowledge. With awareness of nonverbal consciousness, we realize that our thinking is the number one obstacle to spiritual realization.

———

I am an actor. William Shakespeare is not only a great dramatic writer but also a great spiritual thinker. He said that the world is a stage and we are actors on it. This beautiful and profound statement impresses me. I found a similar concept in the spiritual literature of India. In Sanskrit the word *lila* means "play" and is used to describe the creation of the world. Don't you think that these are profound spiritual concepts?
These are indeed beautiful literary and mythological conceptual statements conceived by our creative mental ability. They are concepts in our thinking mind.

Aren't concepts spiritual when they are so deep?
No matter how deep or beautiful, concepts are ideas in our mind, not spiritual realizations.

What is spiritual realization?

Spiritual realization is not about concepts. Spiritual realization is the absence of conceptual preoccupations. A good example of the opposite to spiritual realization is from Shakespeare's "To be or not to be, that is the question," from *Hamlet*, which is a typical conceptual preoccupation. Concepts are obstacles to spiritual realization. Spiritual realization occurs when your attention is inward-oriented. Find the answer to the fundamental question of who the seeker is.

—

I have spent many years in deep, intense thought about spiritual matters. Now I am told that thoughts are not my consciousness. I urgently need to know if it is possible to have any valid thoughts about spiritual realization.

It is not possible to have any valid thoughts about spiritual realization. If it were possible, it would be verbal or mental information confined to our thinking mind. Spiritual realization is the nonverbal realization that thinking is not part of our spiritual constitution and thoughts are not our consciousness.

—

My mind craves spiritual beliefs. Is it possible to live without spiritual beliefs?

You are born without spiritual beliefs. When you realize that spiritual beliefs are not needed, your mind will automatically be busy with useful beliefs.

—

For me, the best way to understand spirituality is through storytelling. But if I understand correctly, any of my thoughts, such as spiritual stories or ideas and concepts or verbal explanations about the world, are only acquired meaningful labels useful mostly for utilitarian matters. All of this is the result of the thinking that occurs in my consciousness, but it is not my consciousness.

Yes.

You say that consciousness is our nonverbal awareness, which we have from birth and at birth.

Yes.

So then what kind of useful information or knowledge do we get from this nonverbal awareness?

Spiritual storytelling is useful. But when you realize that you are nonverbal consciousness, you no longer depend on religious or worldly information for your spiritual wellness. You are no longer controlled by the tyranny of cultural indoctrination.

———

I read that enlightenment is like walking on the edge of a razor. What does this mean?

You need to distinguish between conceptual understanding of the mind and nonverbal realization. Our thinking mind is convinced enlightenment can be understood conceptually. Therefore we need to be super sure that we are not fooled by the mind.

———

Since I discovered that realization is nonconceptual, I became

disappointed and even angry with my guru who taught me conceptual Vedanta for the last twenty years. Although I enjoyed his teaching, I often felt that something was missing. Now I know that his teaching was based on mental understanding. I am eager and ready to have a nonverbal spiritual realization. What shall I do?

If your guru was teaching conceptual Vedanta, he did what he learned from the gurus before him. He is part of religious traditions that are based on conceptual teachings. Such teachings can be a good beginning. The number one requirement to realize nonconceptual spirituality is to find out who you are. When you realize who you are, concepts will be automatically understood as necessary tools for survival. And when this occurs, you will no longer feel that something is missing.

——

I am a scientist and my specialty is astrophysics. I believe in the rational laws of physics, but I also believe in the will of God. Is there a contradiction in my understanding?

There is no contradiction. The will of God and the rational physical laws are mental subjective assumptions that exist in your imagination.

Are you serious?

Where else can your understanding take place? Not in your mind?

Yes, it takes place in my mind, but the laws of physics and God exist in the world outside of me, not in me.

The will of God, world, laws of physics, existence, and outside of you are notions created by the thinking mind, which has the ability to fabricate concepts useful for our survival. Concepts such as the universal laws of physics can have practical application for our survival. Concepts such as the will of God are pure abstract imagination that can be conveniently applied to pacify a restless mind. Nonetheless, these concepts, without exception, are conjured assumptions of the mind. In other words, what we know about the will of God or the laws of physics is subjective. Apart from this subjectivity we know nothing else. As a scientist you know that we see different wavelengths of light as different colors, not as wavelengths of light. One may think that to know they are wavelengths of light is objective, but it is an improved subjective perception. The objective truth is our subjective belief that it is objective. There are no objective perceptions. Our concepts are mental, subjective assumptions. None of them are contradictory. They belong to our imagination.

———

You say in spiritual matters we cannot rely on conceptual information as if it is absolute truth. I understood this a long time ago. Still, the verbal need to know continues to obsess my mind. What did I miss then, and what do I miss now?
Maybe you have a mental understanding that keeps you locked in your mind. For your understanding to be effective, you need to become aware of the relationship between your verbal need to know and your verbal belief in who you think you are. Beliefs are accumulated verbal convictions related to survival. They are not about you, but you think that they are about you. And as long as you believe that this verbal information is about you, your mind will continue believing the verbal information about spirituality. In other words, what you think you are is the direct cause of what you think spirituality ought to be. When you realize that your thoughts about yourself are not you, your mind

will cease obsessing about spiritual thoughts. So find out if your thoughts about you are you. Are you your thoughts?

——

In your explanations about God, you do not make any reference to the positive notions of faith and love. Why is that?
Faith and love are part of the religious belief that God is an outside separate entity. This imaginary mythological belief creates the need for faith and love. My explanations are about how to be aware of our existing innate consciousness, not imagination.

——

I read in the Upanishads that Self-Realization is a condition without thoughts. What does it mean?
It means that realization is nonverbal.

——

I read that all experiences, in the enlightened as well as the ignorant state, that can be described are opposed to our real nature. I have been reading spirituality for a long time, but this statement surprised me. It contradicts much of my understanding of spirituality.
This is a typical statement made by someone aware of their nonverbal consciousness. Most probably you are surprised because you have been reading Vedanta, which is based on conceptual understanding.
Can you explain the difference?
Vedanta is conceptual, based on Hindu mythological beliefs. The

statement you read is written with the awareness that our innate consciousness is nonverbal. It says that our mental achievements are concepts of our mind. Mental descriptions are mental truths.

What is wrong with mental truths?

Nothing is wrong with mental truths. Mental truths are useful and necessary for practical living, but they cannot be applied to describe our real nature. We are born without mental truths. This quote says that mental information has nothing in common with the inherent nonverbal consciousness we are at birth.

What is our real nature?

We are nonverbal consciousness. But to realize this, we first need to find out who we are. The statement you read cannot be fully understood without this realization.

How can I understand who I am?

The understanding of who you are is not intellectual. You need to realize it nonverbally. Ask yourself about who or what this consciousness is that you refer to as *I*. Find this out first.

———

I am worried and afraid of what will happen to me after I die.

Are you also worried about what was happening to you before you were born?

No. I know nothing about what I was before I was born.

You also know nothing about what will happen after you die. Why do you worry about something you know nothing about?

That is my problem. I used to believe I would go to heaven, but now I know this is only imagination. I want to have a believable explanation about what will happen to me after I die. Some spiritual teachers and preachers give beautiful

promises of life after this life. None of these extinguish my anxiety and unbearable feeling of emptiness. I cannot bear being in an unknown void without some belief.

It appears that no ordinary verbal explanation satisfies you. Try a clever explanation. If I tell you that after you die you will be exactly where you were before you were born, would you be happy?

Not really. This explanation gives me nothing to hold on to.

That is good. You no longer easily hold on to any sort of mental explanation. You recognize that heaven is your imagination. But is your conviction that you need to go somewhere after you die not your imagination?

Maybe . . . ?

Your fears about death are also your imagination.

Oh, I see.

So listen carefully. What I am going to tell you may be useful to get you out of the mental trap. Beliefs are based on imagination. Following beliefs dulls our ability to notice the beauty of this world as it is instead of as imagined. Imagination manipulates our thinking. No amount of verbal explanations, however beautiful, can extinguish the feeling of mental emptiness. It is possible that the unease you experience is a sign that you are at the cusp of spiritual nonverbal understanding. Mental emptiness and the feeling of being in the unknown void is a welcome stage prior to spiritual nonverbal awareness. When the mind is empty, what remains is our innate consciousness. This mental emptiness is the unknown about which you complain. But this unknown is not different from the nonverbal consciousness with which you are born.

I miss a believable explanation about who created the universe. Traditionally people hide ignorance of world origin by using the religious concept of God the creator. Science tells us that the origin of the world is due to laws inherent in nature. But this is also another concept. Are we hiding our ignorance behind the laws of nature? Is there a valid answer for our origins that is not just another concept invented by our imagination?

Explanations are conceptual. Realization is nonverbal.

I prefer realization instead of explanations.

So listen carefully. Realization does not propose conceptual explanations for anything and certainly not for our origins. As you implied, concepts cannot provide a satisfactory answer, not even to our intellect. Instead of conceptual answers, nonverbal realization is a direct perception of our existence.

But existence is also just a concept.

Hold on, let me finish. Yes, existence is a concept until you have a direct experience of it without the involvement of your thinking conceptual mind.

How is it possible to have a direct experience?

The direct experience of existence is our own existence. The knowledge that you are or that you exist is innate. You do not have to think about it. It is a direct perception without using your imagination. When you are aware of your own being, your attention stays with the original consciousness you are at birth instead of seeking believable conceptual explanations. Conceptual explanations of any kind are not needed to realize I exist. The *I am* is the nonconceptual direct realization of your origin and the origin of what is.

———

Does interpreting dreams have any value? I am a psychoanalyst.
Dreaming itself has value, but the interpretation of dreams is adding another dream.

I don't follow.
Why is the interpretation of dreams another dream? Listen carefully. The interpretation is performed using your thinking mind. The mind creates a method of interpretation based on our ability to assume, which is our imagination. This imagination is the result of our belief that verbal meanings are realities. This is a made-up fantasy. This fantasy is no different from dreaming. We can label this a dream that occurs in our thoughts while we are awake. Now, why does dreaming have value? Our mind has the ability to scan an unlimited amount of survival possibilities and concerns, which it performs while we are awake or sleeping. Dreams are survival exercises of our utilitarian mind, and this is the value of dreaming.

———

I am seventy-five years old and a spiritual seeker for most of my adult life. You say that spiritual realization is awareness of our innate nonverbal consciousness. This is very convincing and new to me. So I wonder what is the main error that religions and spiritual schools make?
The main error is to rely on our thinking for spiritual knowledge.

———

Why can logical conclusions on the same subject be so conflicting? For example, scientists say the beginning of creation is due to physical laws of nature, and believers say God created

those laws so this beginning is due to God. Both conclusions seem to be logical. Which one is correct? How reliable are logical conclusions?

A logical conclusion can be correct when the premise is based on a reliable assumption. In your example, both the scientists and the believers assume arbitrarily that there is a beginning of the universe. This is a hypothetical assumption without proof. Some scientists and believers say the universe is eternal and there is no beginning. The other random assumption in your example is that the laws of nature and God have an independent existence. Some scientists say the laws of nature are our subjective conceptual interpretations. And some believers say God is within us as our divine consciousness, not as an independent entity separate from us. God the creator of the world is created in our acquired cultural thoughts and exists as an idea in our mind. These divergent opinions are fragmented perceptions, arbitrary assumptions without proof. When we base our reasoning on dubious assumptions, we can expect dubious and conflicting conclusions.

Can logic ever be true?

It can in abstract reasoning—for example, mathematics, where there are no false assumptions.

Would that mean that our day-to-day thinking is unreliable?

Not all of it. It can be reliable in practical matters when the data on which this thinking is based is reliable. Keep in mind that our thinking is an acquired skill for survival. Your conceptual thoughts are reliable and useful in practical matters. Use them to their fullest potential. Conceptual thoughts are useful as speculative exercises, but if you let your scientific or spiritual concepts become frozen as beliefs, you may be polluting your mind with useless and misleading mental concoctions. You do not need to crowd your mind with concepts. Mind free of concepts is nonverbal consciousness. You are born with nonverbal consciousness, without conceptual thoughts. Be in touch with your innate nonverbal consciousness. This is more than enough to have a fulfilling life.

How can I be in touch with this innate nonverbal consciousness?
Find out what this consciousness is that you have had since birth to which you refer as *I*.

—

I have been hearing you say that thinking is not my consciousness and I am not my thoughts, again and again. Is there anything more profound in nonverbal realization?
Personal and world conflicts are caused by the inability to understand that thinking is not my consciousness and I am not my thoughts. This particular realization is the most profound realization. After this single and fundamental realization, everything spiritual becomes known.

—

Starting with Socrates, we have more than two thousand years of recorded intellectual inquiry called philosophy. Does conceptual philosophical inquiry help us understand nonverbal consciousness?
It can be helpful if and when this philosophical inquiry leads to the realization that conceptual knowledge is incomplete and subject to change with each new intellectual understanding. This realization may help us shift our attention to awareness of our innate nonverbal consciousness.

Why are most of us dependent on spiritual authorities?

To understand your question, the inquiry is needed.

What would the inquiry do?

If you do not do the inquiry, you may not know why you think what you think. Inquiry is an important mental function for understanding the composition of our thinking mind.

How so? Can you explain?

For example, with inquiry you ask yourself why you believe in spirituality and why you are convinced that there is God to believe in.

You mean that there is no God?

I mean that if you do not inquire you may not know why you assume that the belief in God is a normal function of your mind. Are you born with this belief?

I am not born with it, but I have the belief in God.

You see, inquiry tells us you are not born with the belief, but you say you have the belief in God. Ask yourself why you have this belief in God. Do you know why?

I hesitate to ask why. I am afraid to question God's existence.

You are not questioning God's existence. You are questioning your own belief in God's existence. You are questioning why you have this belief in your mind, nothing else. This question has nothing to do with God's existence. Your question about why most of us depend on spiritual authorities is a good question. If you keep inquiring, you will understand why most of us depend on some sort of authority. So if we pursue this line of inquiry further, we will find that we have been trained, starting early in life, to follow unproven beliefs created by secular and religious authorities. But we have not been similarly trained to question these various authorities. Questioning is so uncommon to us that we are even afraid to do it. Without this inquiry, which is our ability to inspect our consciousness, we cannot be free from beliefs that are part of our cultural indoctrination. So most of us are brainwashed to believe in spiritual authorities. Belief in authority prevents self-inquiry and is the reason for spiritual ignorance. Spiritual consciousness is void of mental beliefs.

I know that we receive religious indoctrination, but why do you also include secular indoctrination?

We also receive secular indoctrination from sociopolitical authorities such as Adam Smith, Karl Marx, or Confucius, including movements advocating national or racial superiority, materialism, anarchism, communism, capitalism, and other social creeds. Secular authorities brainwash us to follow their belief systems. They are not different from creeds of organized religions.

Some of them have very positive indoctrinations. Many of us have very constructive beliefs.

Yes, we do. Our society vacillates between positive pro-survival beliefs and negative narrow-minded beliefs. Of course it is better to follow constructive beliefs that lead to many benefits in our society, and obviously our secular and religious authorities play a positive role. However, we need to be clear that beliefs, good and bad, prevent us from performing self-inquiry and questioning our cultural indoctrination. Why? Because our attention can be so absorbed by mental beliefs that the idea of inquiry does not arise. It is prudent to conclude that mental beliefs can be detrimental for spiritual realization.

My belief in God prevents God-realization.

Yes.

—

We are used to seeing the world in fragments, so it took me a long time to understand the fundamental scientific concept of space-time or the fourth dimension. This understanding was extremely satisfying. I call this enlightenment. When I heard you say that existence is understood to be undifferentiated but our mind divides existence into fragments we call objects for utilitarian purposes, it took a lot of pondering and reflection to finally understand this. Understanding undifferentiated, nonfragmented existence is one of the most satisfying and gratifying enlightenments in my life. Are these the same as spiritual realizations?

No. These are subtle, refined conceptual understandings useful for our survival.

They are not spiritual enlightenments?

No, they are not spiritual. The understanding of the fourth dimension as time-space and the understanding of undifferentiated existence are positive and useful concepts occurring in your culturally acquired utilitarian thinking mind. These are temporary ideas in your mind. When your attention is absorbed by mental ideas that you rely on, you cannot know what spiritual realization is.

Then what is spiritual realization?

When conceptual understanding, however subtle or refined, is abandoned and no longer relied on, that remaining consciousness is your spiritual realization. This remaining nonverbal consciousness is not part of your culturally acquired utilitarian thinking mind. This is your original and permanent consciousness you have had since birth. The acknowledgment of this innate unaltered consciousness is spiritual realization, also labeled as realization of the nonverbal self.

What can I do to achieve this realization of the nonverbal self?

Out of habit, you still think that you can achieve spiritual realization by doing something with your thinking mind. When you understand that you can no longer rely on your thinking ability for spiritual realization, your attention, by design, remains and stays in your original nonverbal consciousness. You do not need to do anything with your thinking mind. Spiritual realization is the nonmental awareness that you already are the nonverbal self. However, the mind can investigate who is that *I* who wants to achieve this realization.

——

I have studied spiritual literature for many years. The most advanced teachings are available in Hindu scriptures. For example, Krishna said, "Whomsoever one may worship, the worshipper worships me only." I am sure you agree that this statement is one of the most broad-minded beliefs of any religion. Can nonverbal realization bring an end to my endless seeking of God-realization?

I agree that this statement attributed to Krishna is an all-inclusive religious belief. Inquiry into our consciousness can lead to nonverbal realization, but it is not a religion. Nonverbal realization has nothing in common with any beliefs. Let me explain. The inquiry into our consciousness teaches us that thinking is an acquired verbal skill, useful to deal with utilitarian matters, but it is not our consciousness. This skill is not a reliable instrument to acquire valid spiritual knowledge. Through inquiry we realize that our beliefs are based on unquestioned assumptions. For example, how did we learn that God exists, how did we learn that to believe is normal, how did we learn that scriptures contain reliable information about God, and on and on. Those assumptions are ideas that we receive from our society. We were born without those thoughts and without assumptions. Our spiritual seeking can come to a successful end when we turn our attention to ourselves and begin to ask why we believe that to seek God is normal or that scriptures are our spiritual authorities. When this type of questioning starts, it inevitably leads to the final and the most fundamental question, namely, the *who am I* question. No amount of even the most advanced religious beliefs can satisfy our spiritual thirst until we understand who the seeker is. Beliefs are temporary mental appeasements. The knowledge of *who am I* is permanent. Yes, nonverbal realization can bring your long search to an end.

How do I do that?

Ask yourself what or who this consciousness is with which you already are familiar since birth and refer to as *I*. Discover who you are.

———

The idea that our thinking mind can only produce fragmented knowledge is the most important piece of information I got from any spiritual teaching. I agree that the doctrines of our religions as well as our philosophical, psychological, and sociopolitical knowledge are conceptually fragmented and incomplete. I would even go as far as to say that they are no different from mental fictions. If so, can we also conclude that our scientific knowledge is a mental fiction too?

Knowledge, including scientific knowledge, is a subjective

interpretation of information acquired from the collective mental culture we are born into, which is an accumulation of a large quantity of subjective interpretations done over many generations. In practical applications mental knowledge is reliable. But in spiritual matters relying on mental knowledge is understood as nescience, meaning ignorance. If you enjoy stretching the conventional definition of what fiction means, we can accept that science can be labeled as a useful fiction based on incomplete and fragmented knowledge available today.

What then is the complete nonfragmented knowledge?

The direct awareness of our nonverbal consciousness we have by birth is the complete nonfragmented knowledge. When we know this, the mind experiences our innate nonverbal consciousness as unknowing.

———

Most spiritual creeds and organized religions advocate a variety of positive social teachings. Does awareness of nonverbal consciousness benefit society?

The analytical method of self-inquiry into consciousness leads to nonverbal realization. Enlightened individuals benefit society.

———

Is nonverbal realization an experience like the experience of transcendental meditation? Both are referred to as experiences. Is there a difference?

Yes, there is a difference. Listen carefully. The lack of clarity in this matter is due to the limitations of our language, which has evolved to describe and label mental experiences.

Transcendental meditation is a mental experience, soothing to the mind and easily defined verbally. Realization is nonverbal and cannot be described accurately because there are no words in our language to define nonverbal consciousness. Due to this limitation, the word *experience* is often used generically. Realization is not a mental experience that starts and ends like meditation. Realization is the awareness of the permanent nonverbal consciousness with which you are born.

If it is always there, then why do I not feel it?
Your attention is absorbed by your thinking. You are convinced that you can grasp the meaning of nonverbal realization with your ability to think. Your question about the difference between transcendental meditation and realization indicates that you rely on mental experiences.

My transcendental meditation gives me the experience of bliss. Is bliss a mental experience?
Yes, bliss is mental.

Can meditation lead to nonverbal realization?
Yes, it can. When you realize that meditation produces mental experiences, you practice it to benefit your mind. After this understanding, you abandon relying on mental experiences, including bliss, and find yourself in a mental void. You realize that the consciousness witnessing this void is your permanent nonverbal *I*, the nonverbal self. This is nonverbal realization.

———

I read in sacred literature that we need to be detached to lead an enlightened spiritual life. In monastic beliefs and in yoga, there are exercises to train you to control desires and live in the state of detachment. It seems to me that this type of

attitude cultivates unnatural behavior. I resist the idea of detachment with every fiber of my being. What is your position on this matter?

The idea of detachment is a direct threat to our acquired instrument of survival, the mind. Your resistance to the concept of detachment indicates a healthy pro-survival attitude. The practice of detachment is based on the erroneous belief that our thinking ability is our consciousness and this thinking can be improved with better thoughts. Conceptual thinking is incapable of making any lasting spiritual improvements in our innate nonverbal consciousness. Monastic and yogic practices of detachment are meant to ease the restless mind. They need to be practiced continuously to have an effect. Practices of this kind lead to mental appeasements. These appeasements are mental accomplishments that are erroneously believed to be spiritual enlightenments. However, there is reference to nonmental achievements that can occur as a result of self-inquiry. If we realize that we are nonverbal consciousness and our culturally acquired mental ability is no more than an indispensable survival tool, then we become responsible in the use of our mental abilities for utilitarian needs of survival. And at the same time, we become effortlessly detached from relying on our thinking mind for spiritual knowledge.

———

Most of our activities are based on verbal beliefs. How can we function with awareness of nonverbal consciousness that is without beliefs?

Beliefs are necessary for practical activities. Nonverbal realization is necessary for spiritual maturity.

What is the main feature of nonverbal realization that is not present in other spiritual systems?

Some spiritual systems use esoteric language, storytelling, poetry, riddles, or aphorisms. Reasoning is the main feature used to realize our nonverbal consciousness. This reasoning prevents us from yielding to spiritual fantasy.

———

Some scientists warn us that the future development of artificial intelligence will surpass human intelligence and endanger the very existence of humanity. Other scientists say it will produce wisdom, which may render human wisdom redundant. Is it possible that artificial intelligence will replace the need for us to learn about awareness of nonverbal consciousness?

Artificial intelligence is an improved intelligence that utilizes statistical probabilities developed by fragmented human mental intelligence. No doubt, artificial intelligence can help our thinking instrument and can be used to benefit or to harm humanity. Our regular intelligence, the thinking mind, has been doing this from the beginning of time, sometimes to benefit and sometimes to harm us. Artificial intelligence can do the same but more efficiently. The wisdom that artificial intelligence learns is statistical wisdom, which is fragmented, mental, conceptual, and verbal. And yes, artificial intelligence can learn the verbal methodology of inquiry and replace the need for the traditional oral or written instructions. So artificial intelligence can improve and replace our conceptual knowledge. However, artificial intelligence cannot improve or replace the awareness of our innate nonverbal consciousness. Our conceptual mental knowledge is acquired and learnable. But our nonverbal consciousness is not acquired and not learnable. It is within us at birth. Artificial intelligence cannot touch it. To avoid misuse of artificial intelligence in our lives, spiritual maturity and nonverbal wisdom are necessary. The method of rational inquiry into our consciousness can lead to this maturity and wisdom.

—

I clearly understand that the mind needs concepts for survival. But the prerequisite to nonverbal realization is a mind that is empty of conceptual beliefs. I am not sure that I am capable of having an empty mind, but the very idea that such a state is possible makes me extremely happy. I dare not even think how great this bliss can be when I go beyond the thought of an empty mind and reach the empty mind itself. Is it possible that what prevents me from going beyond the idea of empty mind is that I am trapped by ideas such as undifferentiated reality or consciousness is all there is? Why use such absolute concepts at all?

Absolute concepts are used to demonstrate the limitations of fragmented mental concepts present in our cultural beliefs. Verbal statements, such as undifferentiated reality and consciousness is all there is, are not meant to be taken as absolute truths. They are verbal labels. They help us realize that the concepts given to us by our thinking mind are a fragmented diversity, useful in utilitarian matters, not in spiritual matters. On the level of intellectual understanding, we can abolish erroneous concepts with other, better concepts. There is an ancient proverb that says to take out a thorn, a bigger thorn is needed. Our immature mental ideas can be taken out with our absolute ideas. However, even absolute concepts are still nothing more than concepts, and they will interfere with gaining the empty mind you are after. Now, regarding what you said about bliss, I would like to point out that the notion of bliss is a mental concept too. And as long as you pursue this idea and imagine how great it would be to have this bliss, you are blocking the possibility of having the empty mind you want. If you ask yourself about how you know that an empty mind can give you bliss, you realize that bliss is the result of intense mental convictions, similar to intense religious beliefs. It has nothing in common with an empty mind. The condition of an empty mind occurs when bliss and other fantastic conceptual mental convictions are absent.

———

My meditation teacher says we are born alone and die alone. I read in the Upanishads that consciousness alone exists. When I meditate, this is exactly what I feel. I feel alone in the world and at peace with myself. Is this feeling spiritual or mental realization?
The feeling of being alone in the world is a refined, subtle mental realization, which, as you say, you feel during your meditation. It is a conceptual truth of the mind and not spiritual nonverbal realization. The Upanishad statement that consciousness alone exists is an abstract idea used in an absolute sense. Absolute abstractions are intended to take your thinking mind to the limits of conceptual understanding. Beyond this conceptual understanding, there is no aloneness and no plurality. It is the realm of nonverbal awareness where subjective mental truth is irrelevant. Due to our intellectual upbringing, we easily latch on to any new and intriguing concept such as being alone. The habit

of relying on conceptual verbal meanings is firmly ingrained in our minds. Concepts are ideas, nothing more. As long as you rely on the concept of aloneness, your meditation is a form of mental appeasement that you label as I feel at peace with myself. No doubt, meditation is good for the well-being of the mind. If you ask yourself about who feels alone or who feels at peace, this type of self-inquiry may lead you to know who you are. Spiritual maturity depends on knowing who you are.

———

Why are followers of religions sure their creed is absolutely true?
To be mentally sure is due to the lack of self-inquiry.

———

I know that I am not my mind. I know that my thoughts are not my consciousness. I know that thinking cannot give me spiritual realization. I know that the mind is an acquired survival tool. I know that I am born with consciousness but without thoughts. I know that realization is nonverbal. I also know that realization is the same as awareness of my non-verbal consciousness. And here is the crux of my dilemma. I really do not know what nonverbal consciousness is. I want to know what nonverbal consciousness is. Can you tell me?
You cannot know something nonverbal with your intellect. But you can realize it.
How is realization different?
Realization is a form of nonmental understanding. So listen carefully. It is your mind that says I know or I do not know. But there

is someone who knows what your mind says. This someone is your nonverbal consciousness. So ironically, the thing you failed to recognize is precisely your own nonverbal consciousness that you already are from the time of your birth.

———

When I repeat my mantra in meditation, I know that my mind will inevitably go to a very pleasant state of transcendental peace. When I reflect on my awareness of nonverbal consciousness, I do not know where to park my mind. I have no place to go. What do I do with my mind?
Awareness of nonverbal consciousness is not about the temporary mental sensations of transcendental peace that you get during meditation. Inquiry into *who am I* can lead to the nonmental realization of our nonverbal consciousness, which we already are before the formation of our mind. When this is realized, the mind can function well by itself where it is. There is no need to do anything to or with the mind.

———

Can the practice of meditation give spiritual realization?
Meditation can lead to spiritual realization but cannot give it. Spiritual realization is a nonverbal realization, not an experience created by the conceptual meditative mind.
What creates spiritual realization?
Spiritual realization is an awareness of our nonverbal consciousness. If we do not realize this, then the way realization can be brought to our awareness is through I-inquiry.
How is the I-inquiry done?

By asking what is this consciousness with which you are born and to which you refer as *I*. Ask yourself *who am I*.

Is that all?

Yes.

Then why is there such an emphasis on some form of meditation or prayer in all religions?

Repetition of holy names, words, mantras, or prayers by using rosaries or beaded strings conditions our mind to be focused on a mental ideal conceived by our imagination. Such practices have a positive influence on our emotional or psychosomatic well-being. More often than not, such experiences are temporary sensations in the mind triggered by intense convictions or self-suggestions, a form of emotional self-hypnosis, not unlike experiences of religious rapture. Certainly, these experiences can be intense and can easily be understood, although naïvely, as spiritual realizations. They can be positive and beneficial emotional or psychosomatic experiences, but not spiritual realizations. Spiritual realization is not a temporary sensation in the meditative mind. It is a permanent realization of our innate nonverbal consciousness.

So then meditation is just a beneficial training or conditioning of our mind.

Yes.

——

You say that nonverbal consciousness is the same as spiritual realization. How do I get it?

You do not get it. There is no need to get nonverbal consciousness because you are born with it. The nonverbal consciousness with which you are born did not leave you. It is still with you now.

How can I experience it?

Mental realization and mental consciousness can be experienced, but nonverbal consciousness and spiritual realization cannot be experienced. For example, at birth you do not experience nonverbal consciousness. You are nonverbal consciousness. You are nonverbal consciousness now.

———

Socrates said that the unexamined life is not worth living. Although this information is as old as civilization, it continues to be novel for every new generation. Why?

Indoctrination dislodges self-examination.

I do not understand.

Cultural indoctrination gives us the answers about our place in life, so the idea of self-inquiry does not arise.

You mean religious indoctrination?

Yes, religious and also secular, like sociopolitical and scientific indoctrination.

I know what religious indoctrination is. Is there also sociopolitical and scientific indoctrination?

Yes. Our religious beliefs, our social norms and taboos, our political convictions, and our scientific truths constitute our indoctrination specific to our time and our community. It makes no difference if these beliefs and certitudes are true or not. As long as our mind relies on such conditioning, it cannot be free to inquire into itself. This is what I mean by indoctrination dislodges self-examination.

———

Is misinformation or disinformation the same as indoctrination?
The definition of these terms vary, but essentially they stem from the same mental tendency called demagoguery.

In spite of the spiritual teachings from many remarkable enlightened leaders, disinformation existed in the past and exists today as normal. The only change is that after several populist revolutions in the past two centuries, religious indoctrination subsided and political disinformation increased exponentially. Today, at the beginning of the twenty-first century, we are in full-blown disinformation wars between nations. How can being aware of nonverbal consciousness make a difference?
It can make a difference if we realize that relying on new ideas manufactured by our thinking mind is not enough. We need to realize that ideas are not our innate consciousness. When we realize this, we can no longer be manipulated by indoctrination, misinformation, or disinformation.

But this can only happen on the individual level. What about the rest of society?
Start with yourself first.

———

I am eighty-nine years young. I had a very active life and a successful career. I was raised in a nonreligious family. My father used to say that he was not a believer and not an atheist. He called himself an agnostic. But among all the believers, he preferred the atheists. His favorite saying was we should build schools rather than churches. I admired my father. I agreed with him then, and I still agree with him now. Throughout my life I carried an anthropologist's

curiosity about the human race. I had the opportunity to witness many customs and ways of life during my numerous world travels and realized that people still live and behave in immature tribal ways, trapped in cultural lies. There is not a single society that impressed me, including ancient indigenous tribes of the rainforests; contemporary native communities; Buddhist, Hindu, Taoist, Jewish, Muslim, or Christian societies; or communist or capitalistic countries. I am here only because I heard that you say to be aware of nonverbal consciousness involves using a method of inquiry based on reason. Tell me, are religion and spirituality nothing more than a mental concoction, or is there anything religious or spiritual worth knowing before I die? I have no time for any extensive study or practice. It must be short and based on reason, not belief.

I understand. Most religious and spiritual claims are time-honored mental conceptions. You do not have to believe or study or even practice anything whatsoever. Use your reasoning and ask yourself what is this consciousness you were born with eighty-nine years ago. By asking this question you will know who you are, and this is the single awareness worth having before you die.

———

I am frustrated and discouraged. The harder I try to understand what nonverbal consciousness is, the less I understand. I have tried numerous ways to visualize it or to associate it with other similar meanings, without success. I heard you mention nonverbal consciousness many times, but I still cannot grasp the meaning of it. Whenever I think of it, I

draw a blank and see nothing. Really, what exactly is nonverbal consciousness?

You have been exercising your mind in the conceptual field of thinking. You probably think that nonverbal consciousness can be understood as a concept. Think about it. Is it not absurd that you are trying to understand something nonverbal with a concept. The expression nonverbal consciousness is a descriptive label for the state of our awareness. It is not a concept. To understand this, you need to exercise your ability for self-inquiry. So listen carefully. When you draw a blank and see nothing, ask yourself who is the one who knows that you see nothing. What would be your answer?

I am the one who knows that, of course.

Exactly. This *I* is your permanent innate nonverbal consciousness. You do not need to look for nonverbal consciousness. You are nonverbal consciousness. How do we know this? Well, if we continue the inquiry and ask *who am I*, our conceptual thinking mind will not be able to answer this question. It will go blank. That is normal. The mind deals with verbal questions, whereas the *I* is nonverbal. The *who am I* inquiry takes you directly to the nonverbal *I* or nonverbal consciousness. You are nonverbal consciousness.

———

I used to be an atheist. Through self-inquiry I realized that to have a belief in atheism is the same as to have a belief in God. Both are beliefs. Now I feel free from the need to believe and at peace with myself and the universe. Why are we susceptible to religious and secular beliefs?

Our mind is a survival tool that soaks up incredible information.

Our early mental conditioning trained us to believe in unbelievable stories. This makes us susceptible to believe in misinformation.

Why don't we realize that beliefs are dangerous, not only for individual development but also for society at large? How can we have a society that is not raised on fake and useless beliefs?

When you change yourself, you change society. Self-inquiry is the way to prevent being influenced by the political and religious demagoguery inherent in our cultural life. We are nonverbal consciousness. Our innate nonverbal consciousness is not susceptible to useless beliefs.

——

Does the knowledge from nonverbal realization represent absolute truth?

Absolute truth is a mental abstraction that exists in your imagination. The method of self-inquiry to reveal who you are leads to the realization of nonverbal consciousness.

——

You say that we acquire archaic mythological beliefs from our cultural environment. Can you give an example?

Our ancestors attributed godly powers to natural phenomena that they did not understand. To explain those events, they created the idea of God or gods. The need to rely on an external divine power is an archaic mythological belief present in our cultural environment today. We acquire this belief during our upbringing.

Is it important to give up the mind in order to realize nonverbal spiritual truth?

It is for spiritual realization that you give up relying on your thinking mind. You do not give up the mind itself. The mind is valuable and useful. You need a strong and sharp mind for your utilitarian activities.

Humanity has made good progress in scientific research and even in scientific cooperation, but in the sociopolitical area the opposite is true. Since the beginning of recorded history, we are continuously in immature cultural and political conflicts. Why?

Yes, we made some progress in learning how to explore the physical world, but we still did not learn how to explore the world of our own consciousness. Immature conflicts are caused by our deep-rooted cultural misconceptions. Our fundamental misconception is that we believe our ideas represent absolute truth. We do not realize that our ideas are acquired survival tools to deal with practical matters. This understanding, however, is precisely what is needed to have a harmonious collective life.

Could the answer be that simple?

Yes. In present-day civilization, we have been trained how to successfully use our ideas for scientific work. But we have not been instructed what is the composition of our consciousness and what is the place, the role, and the purpose of our ideas in that consciousness. We need to learn that thoughts are acquired tools for survival but not our innate consciousness. We are born without ideas. Until we realize this and abandon our false identification with acquired mental concepts, we will continue using ideas inappropriately and in dangerous ways. For good or bad, ideas are powerful. However, the realization that ideas are useful tools within our consciousness but not consciousness itself is even more powerful. This particular realization is uniquely capable of establishing collective cooperation.

Is there a difference between believing in God and knowing God?
Believing in God is when you think that God is a separate being outside of you. Believing takes place in your thinking mind. Whereas knowing God is when you realize that the consciousness you are born with is God consciousness. The realization of knowing God takes place in your nonverbal consciousness.
And what is the difference between understanding and realization?
Understanding is verbal and realization is nonverbal.

I always had an intuition that the notion we exist as separate independent individuals is a false assumption cultivated for social convenience. I would like to support my intuition with an intellectual explanation. How would you do that?
We have no independent existence. Without other people, plants, animals, insects, bacteria, air, water, sun, moon, planets, stars, galaxies, and everything else in this vast universe, we cannot exist.

—

Spiritual schools are supposed to create special enlightened individuals. What kind of special people are produced by nonverbal realization?

Nonverbal realization produces normal people.

—

When I was a university student, I became disappointed after I read about major organized religions of the world. I had two options: become an atheist or a Deist. I settled for the Jeffersonian-type Deism, and that is what I am today. I heard from you about awareness of nonverbal consciousness. Is it different from Deism?

Yes. Deism is a conceptual belief system based on the assumption that God the creator of the world exists as a separate being. With awareness of nonverbal consciousness, there is no need for conceptual beliefs.

How do you explain the creation of the world?

Your question assumes that there is a creation. It is your thoughts that create the concepts of creation and of God. Thinking is conceptual. It manufactures conceptual questions and also manufactures conceptual answers. This is what Deism does. Thinking is strictly a utilitarian instrument that is incapable of providing reliable spiritual information.

If I understand correctly, the question of creation and the question about God are simply conceptual beliefs.

Yes. Atheism and Deism are not different. Atheists say there is no God, and Deists say there is God. Both are inconsequential beliefs. Now you have a third option. Inquiry into the structure of consciousness leads to freedom from beliefs.

Does freedom from beliefs mean no belief in an external God? Buddhist spirituality has no belief in an external God and is often called spiritual atheism. Can awareness of nonverbal consciousness be called spiritual atheism?

Although it has no belief in external gods or God, a better label for it is spiritual gnosis. Gnosis means nonverbal realization without believing in an external divine entity. The terms *noetic* in philosophy and *apperception* in psychology are used for this type of realization. Similarly, nonverbal realizations of this type are mentioned in Buddhist as well as Hindu, Tao, Christian, Jewish, Sufi, and Shamanic spiritual writings. We are born with divine consciousness, and you can realize this through the inquiry into your consciousness.

So is this my third option?

Yes.

———

You say things I never heard before, like thinking is not our consciousness. How can I be sure that what you are saying is true?

You can be sure that it is true when you verify it through your experience. Ask yourself how did I get all those words and ideas, meaning all those thoughts that make up my mind. Was I born with those thoughts? Inquiry leads to the realization that you are born without thoughts and that thoughts are useful mental survival know-how acquired from the collective cultural environment. There is no thinking in your innate consciousness.

Thinking resides *in* consciousness but it itself is *not* consciousness. Consciousness is without thoughts. You are this nonverbal consciousness now.

——

Tell me in simple words how I can know who I am.
The main obstacle to knowing who we are is the erroneous belief that thinking is our consciousness. Self-inquiry reveals that consciousness is nonverbal, not conditioned by outside civilization and present within us from birth. You are this nonverbal innate consciousness.

——

When I hear about the nonverbal self, I understand it as obvious, but I do not remember this in my daily life.
There is nothing to remember mentally or to mentally know about the nonverbal self. If we know mentally what the self is, then it is another thought, and we are back in the conceptual mind. What the mind can know is what the self is not. For example, the self is not anything that the conceptual mind can possibly know. Awareness of nonverbal self does not need mental help.

——

How can I avoid being indoctrinated by the cultural environment?
The realization that you are nonverbal consciousness is our spiritual maturity as human beings, which influences the progression toward maturity of society at large. This understanding allows

our attention to shift from mental to nonmental awareness, from conceptual mind to nonconceptual mind, which in turn gives us the awareness of undifferentiated reality. Our thinking mind no longer assumes the role of our consciousness. The mind is relegated to its utilitarian function and can no longer be indoctrinated by cultural beliefs.

———

I am intrigued by my attention. What is it?
Our attention is nonverbal consciousness. This ever-present attention, which is zero-thought-consciousness, is our innate awareness. It is also referred to as nonverbal self. I label it holy void. This silent attention, this innate holy void, is our divine consciousness.

———

I love reading about the science of mathematics, which is considered to be the most elegant knowledge. What do you find to be the most elegant aspect of nonverbal realization?
The most elegant aspect is the awareness that we are not our thoughts.

———

The job of my mind is to fragment or differentiate reality. How can I grasp the meaning of undifferentiated reality with my differentiating mind?
You cannot grasp the meaning of undifferentiated reality with your differentiating mind. You are born with nonverbal consciousness

that is undifferentiated reality. Your mind differentiates reality in order to cope with the practical necessities of life.

Early in life I started reading Jewish mystical writings. Later I read Christian and Muslim mystic spirituality. Now I am reading books on Advaita, Buddhism, and Taoism. Although the foundation of these spiritual disciplines seems to be the same, the religions based on them are historically antagonistic to each other. Why?

Historically, most of us believe that our thinking mind is a source of valid spiritual knowledge. We have created religions based on verbal beliefs that differ between social groups. Religions that rely on mental imagination are prone to misunderstanding that can easily lead to conflict, whereas nonverbal consciousness that we are at birth is the same for all of us.

Why do we need inquiry?

We need inquiry to free us from the mental quagmire of false religious, spiritual, and secular beliefs.

You say consciousness is all there is. You also say reality is undifferentiated. Are these not assumptions without proof and part of our mental delusion?

If you understand them as conceptual beliefs in your mind, yes, they are mental delusions. These assumptions are temporary working hypotheses. They are useful in the inquiry process leading to the realization that we are nonverbal consciousness.

—

It seems that I have been scouring the spiritual horizon forever looking for enlightenment. I read an infinite number of fantastic descriptions of spiritual enlightenment, and I am not enlightened. You say the direct awareness of nonverbal consciousness is enlightenment. What does it mean?
The direct awareness of nonverbal consciousness is experienced by each one of us as our attention. Take your attention off reading and put it on your attention. Your attention is nonverbal. The realization that our attention is the divine nonverbal consciousness with which we are born is spiritual enlightenment.

—

You say awareness of our nonverbal consciousness is enlightenment. We are born with nonverbal consciousness. It is not a thought, not a myth, but a presence. We experience it concretely as our attention. It is our mute higher self, which you call nonverbal self. It is the ever-present nonverbal *I*. It is divine and God-given. But we know that the word *nonverbal* means not knowable by our mind. So in essence, you are saying not to know is to know. Therefore, in this context, can we also say not to know is enlightenment?
Yes. We can say that.

—

Your explanations about enlightenment are too complicated and make no sense. Can you tell me in ordinary words what is enlightenment?

Yes. Enlightenment is the realization that our culturally acquired mental spiritual beliefs are superstitions.

—

Years ago when I started reading about spirituality, I came across a curious statement supposedly written thousands of years ago. It said that only one in a million can be spiritually enlightened. Why?

Very few people realize that thinking is not consciousness.

—

You say that awareness of our innate nonverbal consciousness frees us from the tyranny of thought. What is tyranny of thought?

Relying on thoughts as true in religious and spiritual matters leads to fanaticism and falsehoods and in sociopolitical matters leads to conflict and war. This is what is meant by tyranny of thought.

What about relying on thoughts in science?

In utilitarian and scientific matters, relying on thoughts creates better survival conditions. When we are aware of our innate nonverbal consciousness, we realize that thoughts are acquired useful mental skills, *not* our consciousness. This realization frees us from the tyranny of thought.

—

I asked you this before, but I did not understand your answer. Can you explain again what is the reason that it is not necessary to have a guru to gain spiritual realization?

It is possible to follow a guru when we think that spiritual realization is verbal and can be gained conceptually with our thinking ability. A guru or any spiritual leader can entertain you with holy tales and convincing ideological explanations that satisfy and gratify your mind. However, this type of information is verbal spirituality based on mental beliefs, no different from any religion that keeps your understanding confined to the realm of ideas. The moment you realize that spiritual knowledge is nonverbal and realization is awareness of your ever-present innate nonverbal consciousness, you will know precisely why you have no need for any spiritual authority. You become a guru to yourself.

———

You say the influence of mythology extends into our ordinary daily beliefs that we never question. How can I identify my mythological beliefs?

The *who am I* inquiry leads to the realization that you are born without beliefs and with a consciousness that is nonverbal. You acquire words and beliefs from the collective cultural environment. Your mind is composed of acquired survival information; social skills; and also religious, spiritual, and secular mythological superstitions. Use inquiry to learn about the composition of your mind and to identify mythological beliefs.

———

You speak of nonverbal awareness, which you refer to as our natural state. Natural state has been discussed throughout history. For example, in antiquity we had Socrates, who said that wisdom and intelligence are innate or natural in man, then Jean Jacques Rousseau, the eighteenth-century Enlightenment philosopher, spoke of natural man. Although this point of view is interesting, history does not pay attention to it. What is important to us are ideas from people such as the Roman emperor Julius Caesar, who wrote about his military conquests; Adam Smith and Karl Marx, who wrote about economic principles; or Arthur C. Clarke, who proposed scientific ideas for satellite communication and space exploration. These individuals have concrete, useful ideas that are not about nonverbal consciousness. Here is my question. Since we are destined to become a galactic civilization, is it not wasteful to be overly concerned with nonverbal consciousness instead of channeling our energy to formulate futuristic ideas for a new civilization?

Throughout history, mental ideas and spiritual awareness coexist side by side. We emphasize the nonverbal aspect of consciousness that is neglected in our predominantly intellectual cultures. Through inquiry we realize that ideas are means, not goals. Ideas by themselves are impotent, but if used as goals, they can either be beneficial or detrimental. Whereas when ideas are understood as part of our acquired thinking mind, they can be used effectively as what they are, utilitarian tools. We utilize an aptitude based on logic to inquire into consciousness. The role of inquiry is to free us from the limitations of archaic cultural conditioning. When we realize that human beings and other forms of life are sacred nonverbal consciousness and our conceptual ideas are an acquired extraordinary skill meant to be used for the survival of life, our chances for a positive evolution toward a futuristic civilization will be increased exponentially. We are an integral part of biological diversity of life. If we use our ideas for anything other than the preservation of diversity, we harm ourselves. The condition of our civilization depends on the quality of awareness in each one of us. Realizing the vital role of both the nonverbal and the mental aspect of consciousness is necessary to function in our present-day civilization and will probably also be necessary in the futuristic galactic civilization that you imagine to be our destiny.

—

Are religious beliefs superstitions?
Can we assume that you did not create those beliefs yourself, but you received them from the society you live in?
Yes, that is correct.
Those culturally acquired religious beliefs are riddled with archaic misconceptions and inconsistent with rational thought. So they are defined as superstitions.

—

You say that awareness of our nonverbal consciousness occurs when we put attention on our attention. Can you tell me how to do this?
Close your eyes and put your attention inside. Are you aware that you are conscious?
Yes, I am.
This consciousness is your nonverbal consciousness.

What is nonverbal consciousness, and why is it important to be aware of it?

Nonverbal consciousness is the consciousness we have at birth. The awareness of it is important because this innate nonverbal consciousness is our source of wisdom.

What kind of wisdom is it?

This wisdom is the perception of our world without words.

I thought that wisdom is expressed in words, like in the scriptures—for example, love thy enemy like yourself.

This statement is a product of our thoughts that fragment our world into concepts. The assumption that there are enemies and friends leads to conflict. When we view the world with the awareness of our innate nonverbal consciousness, we realize that wisdom is nonverbal.

I understand that the mind is in consciousness and consciousness is in me. But who is me?

The mind is in consciousness. But consciousness is not in you. You are consciousness.

Although I am born with nonverbal consciousness, I do not know how to be aware of it.

It is your mind that is saying I do not know how. There is someone who is aware of what your mind is saying. This someone is the nonverbal consciousness with which you are born.

226

—

I like to read ancient Greek philosophy where metaphysical explanations are better than anywhere else. But you say that the awareness of our nonverbal consciousness gives us metaphysical knowledge. Can you explain?

Nonverbal consciousness is metaphysical consciousness. You are born with it.

—

You say that without inquiry we will spend our life in a state of mental delusion. What exactly is mental delusion?

Mental delusion is the belief that our thinking mind can give us spiritual knowledge. We are raised with this misconception.

If this is so, our upbringing keeps us in a mental delusion.

Yes, exactly.

Is this why we need inquiry?

Yes. Inquiry shows us that the belief thinking can give us spiritual realization is false. We are born with spiritual consciousness that is without thoughts. During our upbringing we acquire thinking, a mental skill specifically meant to deal with practical survival needs. When we rely on thinking for spiritual knowledge, we are in a state of mental delusion. With this realization, mental delusion ends.

ABOUT THE AUTHOR

Yarek was born near Wilejka, Poland, an area that Stalin would soon invade and turn into a Soviet Socialist Republic. Yarek was three years old and at home on Christmas playing with two wolf puppies his father had found abandoned in the forest. Suddenly there was a loud knock at the door. The armed men outside announced that the entire family was being deported to a Siberian Gulag and had two hours to collect any belongings they wanted to bring. His family spent the next two and a half years as Gulag prisoners.

When Hitler attacked Russia, Winston Churchill sent General Anders to negotiate the release of all Gulag prisoners of Polish descent in exchange for the formation of a Polish army that would help Stalin defend Russia against Hitler. Once released, Yarek, along with his brother and mother, was sent to live in a British colony in Tanzania while his father fought in World War II for six years. Yarek loved his time in Africa; the Tanzanian people introduced him to a more relaxed lifestyle in harmony with nature and their community. So by the time he was twelve years old, Yarek had experienced two opposite extremes of human behavior.

He received his bachelor of science degree from the University of Paris in France. His master of arts in philosophy is from the University of Madras in India. There he researched Advaita philosophy under the mentorship of Professor T.M.P. Mahadevan, who was considered the world's leading authority on the subject. His unusual childhood experiences left Yarek with unanswered questions. He stopped digging through the ancient archives in Madras only after he knew that he had found all the pieces necessary to answer his own questions. Decades would pass before he wrote *HOLY VOID: Zero-Thought-Consciousness*.

While Yarek was a graduate student in the University of Madras's philosophy department for five years, he lived in a villa at the Theosophical Society's headquarters. There he became close friends with Wanda Dynowska, a.k.a. "Umadevi," and Maurice Frydman, a.k.a. "Bharatananda." Through Umadevi and Bharatananda, Yarek got to know Jiddu Krishnamurti and Terence Gray (a.k.a. Wei Wu Wei) in Switzerland and His Holiness the Dalai Lama in Dharamsala.

After Yarek completed his research, Umadevi and Bharatananda arranged speaking engagements for him through their contacts in Europe and the United States. Yarek was invited to speak at gatherings of people interested in consciousness and spirituality. He spoke in Paris, Brussels, New York, and Los Angeles. At each event he included time for discussion and questions. He also taught philosophy at the University of California, Santa Cruz. Through these events he learned to understand the needs, interests, and misconceptions people have about consciousness and enlightenment.

Although his interest in consciousness lasted his entire life, he simultaneously had a long career as an artist, mostly as a motion-picture sculptor on movies produced by major studios in Hollywood including *Jurassic Park III*, *Batman and Robin*, *Batman Forever*, *Jurassic Park*, *Bram Stoker's Dracula*, and forty other films. He also was an artist and sculptor in Europe and the United States. He met his wife in 1988 after he turned his attention to the consciousness he had since birth. He knew she was the one the moment he heard her voice.